C-Desk Technology

Flexible Shift Working

A New Approach to Flexible Shift Working using Banked Hours

Not Ready-Made Shift Patterns,

Shift Patterns Made to Measure

Dr Angela Moore

Alec Jezewski

Published by C-Desk Technology 2023

Copyright © C-Desk Technology 2023

First published in Great Britain in 2023

C-Desk Technology

The Old Vicarage, Station Road, Rolleston, Newark, Nottinghamshire, Great Britain, NG23 5SE

www.visualrota.co.uk

www.oranalysts.com

dr-moore.thinkific.com

ISBN: 9798854042956

Contents

Introduction

When your organisation next undertakes a review of their operation or introduces a new operation, try to include flexible working as the solution to common problems everyone has. This book is about using Banked Hours as part of the overall solution to create a more efficient and effective operation.

Flexible working is about matching demand. This means that no one is ever over or underworked. Most workforces are continually fluctuating as holidays, absence and training take people away from their duties. At the same time, few operations have a stable demand. For most people demand will fluctuate hourly, daily, weekly, or annually. To match the workforce to your demand you need a flexible approach. Banked Hours is a great way to improve your flexibility. They maintain operations with relatively little day-to-day input from managers and at a fixed cost.

This book is aimed at all types of organisation, be they public bodies, emergency services, the business community and students aiming to be managers. We include examples from our case files involving: call centres, Police, food, pharma, chemicals, health, electronics, security, IT, newspapers, printing, aerospace, energy, banking, mining, engineering, supply chain, logistics, universities and public bodies. We have worked with employers of traffic wardens and satellite controllers. Our fields of expertise include IT control centres, automation, lean and continuous improvement, sustainability, quality control, packaging and innovation.

Flexible working is always desirable for employees and managers. Being more flexible means that the company can achieve greater efficiency and the employees can get time off when they want it.

Many offices will be familiar with "Flexi Time". Flexi Time allows the employee to work at a time of their choosing within the company's rules. This means that by working more hours together, they can have more time off together. By more time off, we actually mean more days off. They are perfectly entitled to these extra days off, they are working their contracted hours, they are fulfilling their contract to do the work they are being paid for. The advantages to the employer are even more than those to the employee.

Flexible working is about ensuring that everyone achieves a good work/life balance. To do this we need to ensure that all of the shifts are correctly staffed. Not having the right people, with the right skills puts undue pressure on to people. It creates stress for the shift workers but especially their managers. Being correctly staffed ensures that no one is under or over worked, thus reducing the stress at work. The shift pattern should be based around creating a stable environment for shift workers. The premise is to prevent nepotism, favoritism, harassment or bullying. To think of the team as a family and to actively encourage cross team integration through the cover shift program to maintain a stable operation.

When it comes to flexible shift work it is not enough to just have one tool at your disposal. A good manager needs lots of tools available for all eventualities. A good manager will have backup plans for alternative scenarios thus they will never have to fall back on firefighting every problem as it occurs.

Banked Hours is great at managing flexible demand and improving shift worker's work/life balance. However, you should run a Banked Hours system with at least a few other flexibility tools.

Office Staff

Office staff are very different to shift workers. In general, office staff work the same set hours Monday to Friday. This is the traditional way of working. "Flexi Time" breaks this assumption. Not all work has to be done Monday to Friday. Not all work has to be done between 9-5. To have flexibility, you need to increase the available working time, say 7am to 7pm.

The point you should be noting is that, first of all, most office work is not time critical, by that I do not mean that they do not have to meet deadlines, rather they can do the work just as effectively at 7a.m. as at 9a.m. most of the time.

The advantages of Flexi Time

Benefits for the individual;

- There is a better work-life balance,
- Fewer commutes,
- Less fatigue,
- More days off,
- Lower sickness,
- Self-motivated working

Benefits for the company;

- Better motivated workers,
- More efficient and effective operation,
- Less fatigued workers, so less errors,
- They have people working overtime hours without paying overtime rates,
- Fewer facilities required, but over a longer time period,
- Lower sickness

Put like that the real question is why isn't everyone doing it?

We promote flexi time to our clients if it is appropriate because the benefits to both parties, far outweigh the disadvantages. In the individual's case, the usual disadvantage is that it means they won't get as much overtime pay, and the company must also ensure that the system is not abused.

Shift Workers

Shift work with Flexi Time is a little more complicated. How do you allow staff to have flexibility when you need them at set times? Shift work means that with the right shift pattern you could get over 10 weeks off per year. We have set up shift patterns where a three-month holiday is possible.

Employees contract with the company to supply a certain number of working hours per week or per year. These are referred to as Contracted Working Hours. The company then has control of these hours to say when and how they will be used. In general, a company will allocate all of these to the shift pattern. However, they don't have to. For countries that set a limit of, say, 40 hours per week, please see chapter on Union Negotiation.

The company can instead decide to set up a Bank. This Bank contains a number of prepaid-for hours. So, the employees Contracted Working Hours are then split between the shift pattern and The Bank. This creates flexibility as you then have hours, pre-paid-for hours, at your disposal.

The company allocates most of the contracted working hours into a shift pattern that requires staff to turn up for work at a certain time and date, and the remaining hours go into The Bank. Typically, 5-10% of Contracted Working Hours are allocated to The Bank. The hours in The Bank are specifically allocated to a person, and every person can have a different number of hours in their Bank.

The company can then utilise those "Banked" hours in any way agreed with the staff. This allows the company to roster in the Banked hours at any time in the year without having to plan the entire year before issuing the shift pattern.

Banked Hours works for a company as long as the company does **not** abuse it. It is a very good method of guaranteeing *Continuity Of Operations*, stability in other words, with minimum effort on both sides.

This book looks at improving the work/life balance of shift workers through greater flexibility. As a byproduct, the company can also achieve greater efficiency, reduce costs and increase stability.

Flexibility Methods

When it comes to shift working, what you want is the right people, in the right place, at the right time. Allowing people to take time off when they want is at odds with this philosophy. Hence most shift patterns are either very rigid or created only days in advance. An inflexible system is expensive as it cannot adapt to change. A manager is left to firefight each case, with one arm tied, or suffer the consequences.

A shift pattern that is created only days in advance is impractical for most people and leaves shift workers feeling like they have very little control over their lives. Thus, they have a very poor work/life balance as they do not know from one week to the next when or even if they will be working.

What you need is a practical approach which allows you and your shift workers to have **flexibility** when needed and **security**.

The best system for achieving flexibility and security is Banked Hours. This creates security for over 90% of the time and flexibility for up to 10% of the time. Thus creating the prefect balance. However, there are other systems available.

Variable Shift Length

Shifts do not all have to be the same length. You can have flexibility through utilising longer and shorter shifts as needed. Short shifts can be flexed up (extend the shift length) to cover for variations in workload and long shifts can be flexed down (reduce the shift length) when not needed.

This means that people know what days they will be working, they just don't know the exact shift length. If you have some set shifts (where you can't change the shift length) with some flexible shifts (where you can change the shift length as needed) you can have a flexible arrangement that gives stability and flexibility.

Shift Swapping

Shift Swapping is when you allow your staff to swap shifts subject to management approval. This means that if your shift workers would like a different day off or prefer to work afternoons as opposed to early shifts, they can swap between themselves. Thus, your employees come to you with solutions not problems.

This also means that not only does every one achieve a better work/life balance by working when they want, but also greater flexibility. So, if they need time off for a child's play, visit the vets or the bank, they no longer need to book a holiday. Instead they simply swap shifts.

Holidays Included

Holidays Included shift patterns are when the holidays are incorporated into the shift pattern. This improves the efficiency of the operation.

You can then use shift swapping to allow shift workers to pick and choose their holidays. What you are presenting them with is a default holiday plan for the year. This means that if they choose to do nothing, they will have good quality time off throughout the year. However if they would like a different holiday they can swap with other people on the shift pattern, and create their own personal shift pattern with the days off they want.

Some employers who are not used to holidays included see this approach as too restrictive. They want to allow their employees greater flexibility whilst taking advantage of the holidays included benefits. They therefore only include about 75-90% of the holidays in the shift pattern and then allow their shift workers to "pick" their other holidays in accordance with standard holiday rules.

These holidays which are not included in the shift pattern are called Floating Days or Golden Days. These are days that the shift worker can select to have off and the manager has to find a way of covering.

Job and Knock

There is a saying, "Job and Knock" which means that you do the job and then knock off work. It's an old saying for workers who are paid to do a job, not paid for the amount of time they are at work. Hence when they have finished the work, they are free to go home.

You can use this method of working when you don't know the length of a job. Let's say we are discussing repair jobs, the average time it takes to go out and do a "job" is five hours. Hence in an 8-hour shift you can do one job on average, on a 10-hour shift you could do two jobs. On a 12-hour shift you could still do two jobs on average.

Multi-Skilling

Having people with several skills means that there is greater flexibility. Suddenly everyone can cover for everyone else. So, ensuring that you have the right skills is no longer critical, as everyone has the right skills.

This is not always possible where there are highly skilled key workers who require years (if not decades) of training and experience. However, you can use a training matrix and train people in a secondary skill. Hence everyone cannot do every job, but everyone can do at least two jobs. This means that you create a cascade effect where the replacement does the lowest skilled job. Thus, increasing flexibility.

Staggered Lunch Breaks

Staggering breaks is easy; you need to build in the breaks as part of the planning process when managing the workload. Sometimes you could say that breaks will be taken as the workload allows. This works well with responsible staff and an unpredictable workload. Most workloads are predictable. So breaks can be worked in during the slow periods so that all staff are well rested and ready to work during the busy periods.

Staggered Starts

Not everyone has to start at the same time. In the past this was frowned upon and old school managers dislike it. If everyone comes into work at the same time, it's easy to see who is on time and who is late. If you have staggered starts it's not so easy to see if people are late. You also get a 'them and us' resentment;

'why do they get the start late?' 'Why do they get to go home early?'

However if you use staggered starts they are very effective when it comes to matching the workload.

They are also very useful for eliminating handover and issues associated with handovers.

U-Shifts

U-shifts are when you incorporate *Unallocated* shifts into the shift pattern. These U-Shifts can be used to flex up when you have extra work. Flex up as in bring people into work. They can be flexed down, as in send people home when you don't need them.

Hence the vast majority of their shifts are known in advance. They also know when they have a guaranteed day off. What they don't know (often until the day) is what they will be working when they are scheduled for a U-shift.

Run Short

Running short (trying to run the operation with less people than is needed) is everyone's worse scenario. For management they are worried about meeting deadlines. For employees they are faced with having to work harder, which is more stressful and fatiguing. Therefore, most managers will avoid it at all costs.

However, the ability to run short means that you have far greater flexibility. Having a plan in place where you can reduce output when people are absent, means that you are not having to firefight on the day. Moving an employee from one job to another can mean that one, or both, jobs will run short and this can affect what happens on the next shift.

It helps the decision making process if you separate out the work into work that has to be completed each shift and work that can be delayed or canceled if needed.

Overtime

Overtime is normally the go-to flexible response of managers. Managers know and understand it. It's like a hammer, at university I was always taught if you only have a hammer, you will only ever use a hammer regardless of the problem. However, if you have a full toolset then you use the tool which is most appropriate to the situation.

Most managers only have overtime available to them to cover everything. Hence it is used inappropriately, and results is creating an overtime culture.

When used strategically, overtime is an amazing tool. However, if it is abused it results in high costs, little flexibility and a poor work/life balance.

Agency and Temporary workforce

Agency staff have long been used for office staff because if everyone is working every day, then there is no one to come in and cover for absence. Therefore many businesses rely on agency staff to boost numbers.

There are a lot of costs associated with employing extra headcount. Therefore agency staff are often cheaper, even if the hourly rate is more expensive.

Temporary staff are great for covering holidays. Holidays are known about a long time in advance and students are available during peak times. Therefore they are the perfect match. Students are cheap, they are intelligent and can bring the latest idea into the business. If you use those studying to be doctors and those going on to post graduate degrees, then you can use them for longer than the basic three years. So if you train them in their first year, they can come back every year they are studying with minimal training costs.

Ideally you would get everyone's holiday requests in early for the summer, Easter and Christmas holidays they want. Then contact all of your temporary staff, asking which shifts they would be willing to cover. Then you can allow holidays only after they have been covered. This means that you are always correctly staffed with the minimum of disruption. The students also know what they will be working in advance and their pay.

Stepping down

Very often the only person you can rely on at short notice, is yourself. So a common practice is for managers to step down and fill in. Managers are often expected to work at the weekends and during peak holiday seasons. They are the last resort.

Banked Hours

Banked Hours is where people are paid in advance to work when needed. In practice about 90% of their hours are scheduled into the shift pattern. Around 10% (the exact number of hours is based on the requirements) is reserved to be used as the company needs them. It is very beneficial to both the employer and employee when used correctly. Unfortunately it is very easy to miss use and is open to abuse by managers and shift workers. So a lot of this book is about how to use it correctly without abusing trust. The manager trusts the employee to come in when needed and the employee trust the manager to only bring them in when needed.

Summary

There are 12 different ways of working flexibly:

- Variable Shift Length
- Shift Swapping
- Holidays Included
- Job and Knock
- Multi-Skilling
- Staggered Lunch Breaks
- Staggered Starts
- U-Shifts
- Run Short
- Overtime
- Agency and Temporary workforce
- Stepping down
- Banked Hours

Having a flexible option helps everyone from customers to managers to employees. Flexible working allows you to respond quicker to change, ensure employees are not overworked or bored, meet customer needs and deadlines and do it at a lower cost.

Banked Hours

Banked Hours system is a great scheme that allows an employer to call in staff when needed. Bank Hours or Reserved Hours are the terms used to reference a particular technique of flexible working. The Banked Hours are set up as a means of running an operation without staff having to work additional hours outside their normal contractual hours. The operation can be 24/365, or Office Hours, or anything in-between. They can be used with part-time staff and full-time staff. They are to cover all eventualities that could cause the Operation to fail, typically absences.

The Banked Hours are set up to minimise disruption to all the staff by sharing out the disruption among all the staff in a controlled manner.

Bank Hours are to cover for;

- Holidays,
- Absences,
- Training,
- Leave,
- Ad-hoc workloads,
- Variations in workloads,
- Leavers,
- Step-ups and step-downs,
- Secondments,
- Meetings.

Key Benefits

For the company the benefits of Banked Hours are obvious. They can ensure *modus operandi* is maintained at all times. This means that they can ensure that they will always have the correct skills, when and where they need them. They can plan work. Therefore, they can guarantee that they can meet deadlines, and achieve SLA's. Reduce absence. Fit in training, ad-hoc work and cover for absence within the contract hours.

All in all, a Banked Hours scheme means that the operation is more efficient and less stressful for everyone.

Unfortunately benefits to the company rarely hold any sway with the shift workers. Telling them that they should adopt this new way of working because it will be more efficient is often viewed as a cost-saving scheme that will ultimately lead to downsizing and loss of income. This is especially true of high overtime earners.

Selling a new idea is always difficult. People are scared of change. They don't understand it and are always afraid that things will be worse on the new system compared to the last. So when it comes to Banked Hours you need to have all of the answers at your fingertips to show people that there is nothing to be scared of. This proves to them that you have thought about the problem and have a solution.

Managers and workers not eligible for overtime payment

There are many management grades who's T&Cs do not allow them to work overtime. This can result in a loss in pay if they are promoted. Any extra hours they work do not receive any additional rewards.

We have found that Banked Hours is an ideal solution. The managers can have a number of hours reserved at the start of the year to cover for contingencies. These can include; sickness, leave, ad-hoc work, deadlines, etc.

This works by rostering in days off at the start of the year to create the Banked Hours. So, if they should be scheduled for 208 shifts each year, we schedule them for 195 shifts and keep back 13 shifts. This gives them 13 extra days off initially.

For one company where the managers were on a Banked Hours system, it resulted in management absences falling to zero: and they were always correctly staffed. The managers made arrangements ahead of time for any contingencies so they didn't have to work any additional days as no one was ever 'absent'.. It also helps with deadlines and time management skills.

So how do you sell a new way of working that has clear benefits to the company?

Banked Hours is all about work/life balance. The shift workers are better off with Banked Hours. However, the benefits are dependent on the system and the situation.

Not everyone needs to be on the Banked Hours scheme. Therefore, if you fail to convince everyone at the start that Banked Hours is to their benefit, you can start by asking for volunteers. Provided that you have a large enough group of volunteers, you can run the Banked Hours system.

This book contains an example where everyone, 100%, works Banked Hours and then this is compared to only 50% or 25% of employees working on Banked Hours.

Being able to see the system in operation is far more convincing than management telling staff of the benefits. It does take time for people to see the benefits. Because the Banked Hours are usually written off at the end of the year, it will take at least one year for people to witness the benefits. Less stress and more time off.

Unfortunately there are some people who will only ever see the negatives of any system. For Banked Hours, they see it as always having to be at the company's beck and call. Until they experience the positives, the extra time off, etc. It is rather like a person who sees eating out in a restaurant as a needless expense. Until they experience what it is like, they can't understand why you would do it as it's more expensive than eating at home.

However new starters are merely recruited on to the Banked Hours scheme and the people who don't want to work it are gradually phased out due to natural turnover or they request to enjoy the benefits that their colleagues enjoy.

The main benefits to the shift workers for Banked Hours are:

- Extra paid time off
- Less working time
- Less stress
- Easier work
- Planned cover arrangements
- Flat pay to help with budgeting
- Golden Days
- Guaranteed training
- Guaranteed days off
- Guaranteed holidays
- Fairness
- Not being contacted by work on their days off
- Not being over worked
- More weekends off
- Pre-arranged cover for when they or their colleagues are absent
- Improved work/life balance
- Can be used to alter working patterns when overtime is not allowed
- Reduction in disruption caused by absence

If we look at a typical 24/365 shift operation, we can look at the benefits to the employee. If we have 10 people on a shift, say a production line, and one person goes off sick and is not replaced. Everyone is now rearranged to keep the line going, the line isn't going to stop due to an absent colleague. This means rearranging the jobs continually through the shift, moving break times, losing bonus payments if the line underproduces, and a lot of running around for everyone. If the initial schedule was for 180 shifts each with 10 people and an absence rate of 3%, then we can expect 47 with a sickness absence and 133 shifts with everyone there.

The cover arrangement might be on 17 occasions with about 8 call-ins over the year. Each call in will be known about 12 to 24 hours, or more, in advance. In exchange for having 180 stress-free shifts, there will be 8 occasions of work and 9 extra days off a year, about 2 weeks of extra time off.

Creating Banked Hours

Bank Hours can be a portion of the normal contracted hours. However, you can also purchase Bank Hours, which are in addition to the normal contracted hours. Often it is a combination of the two.

For example, staff are on a 24/365 Holidays Included Shift Pattern (HISP) organised as 5 teams. Their contract hours are 40 hours per week and they have an annual holiday entitlement of 5 weeks (25 days) and 8 Bank Holidays each of 8 hours. Their equivalent annual hours are 40x52 = 2,080 hours per year and the annual holiday is 33x8 = 264 hours per year. This makes their annual contracted working hours 2,080-264 = 1,816 hours per year. The HISP schedules them to work 1,752hours per year. The difference between their annual contracted working hours and their scheduled hours is 1,816-1,752 = 64 hours. The 64 hours are hours that should be worked but do not need to be scheduled as a part of the normal operation. These 64 hours are then moved to the Bank for use at a later time.

If our calculations on the number of Bank Hours showed we actually needed 100 hours, then we would need to create 36 more hours to make up the shortfall. The usual method is to purchase these hours, if possible at a basic hourly rate, but often at an overtime rate.

Shutdowns should be included in any calculation. So, in the above example, if the operation was to shut down for 72 hours over Christmas, then the calculation for the annual working hours of the HISP would be 24x362 = 8,688 hours per year. This split over the 5 teams is 1,738 hours each. This would create a Bank of 1,818-1,738 = 80 hours per year.

Purchasing Banked Hours

If the basic hours do not provide sufficient Banked Hours and they need to be purchased, the question is; how much will they cost. In situations where staff are on a 'no overtime' contract, then either all the hours in a Bank have to be part of their basic hours or they will have to work any additional hours without payment. For the majority of staff, who are eligible for overtime, then they would expect any additional hours they work to be paid for at overtime rates.

Many organisations have several overtime rates applicable for different times of the day or week or both. In that case, a composite overtime rate can be created. For example, if the overtime rate is time+50% for all overtime except for Sundays, which is at time+100%, then we can use 6/7th of 50% and 1/7th of 100% to arrive at a composite rate of 57%. This is based on there being an equal probability of using the Banked Hours at any time.

However, it can be argued that a different criteria is used, such as the likelihood of all the hours being used, or whether additional hours have been included for rare events, or that training takes place during office hours. These logical arguments should serve to reduce the cost of the Banked Hours.

Budgetary Considerations for the Company

The Banked Hours system is not necessarily the cheapest option; however it does provide a guarantee of the continuity of the Operation for a fixed budget. The cheapest option would probably be Annualised Hours with TOIL (Time Off In Lieu) for each working hour used for covering absences, etc. with the TOIL being fitted in during downtime. However, that is very inconvenient to the staff and requires daily management judgments on sending staff home. The Banked Hours option is a relatively cheap method of ensuring continuity of Operation if it is set at the right level of hours, and if the Carry Over clause applies, it is quite efficient. However, the right to Carry Over unused hours is rarely conceded in negotiations with Unions and staff.

A key consideration is whether the Banked Hours are at single rate and whether the Shift Allowance applies to these hours. If they are paid for, in advance, at Overtime Rates, then they become a more expensive option than using pure overtime to cover for absences, etc. albeit at a fixed budget known in advance. However using purely overtime on a voluntary basis runs the risk that no one wants to work on Saturday Nights, for instance.

Budgetary Considerations for the Staff

Staff have mixed feelings about Banked Hours and require many reassurances about how it works in practice. On the one hand, it is inconvenient and probably results in unfairness as some staff end up working more hours than other staff, this is the 'glass half empty' feeling. On the other hand, if no one is ill then they end up with more time off, perhaps an extra 2-4 weeks of time off, this is the 'glass half full' feeling.

To be a successful system, it needs to be a continuing practice agreeable to all parties. That means that each year the staff need to see they have some hours left in the Bank, but the company needs to see that it isn't too many and if the company looks back over the last year and says 'absence problems? What absence problems?' then it has worked for both parties.

Banked Hours and Ad-hoc Workloads

Most companies rely on overtime to cover for ad-hoc workloads. So, a system that allows them to bring in people at basic hours is great for the company but could mean a loss in pay for the shift workers. However, there are lots of other benefits.

If overtime is not contractual, then it can be taken away at any time. So, while overtime is a great boost to people's income in the short term, it is not a long-term option. Whereas Banked Hours is designed to be maintained year on year. The peaks and troughs in the workload which make budgeting on overtime difficult are taken out with Banked Hours. With Banked Hours they are paid the same per month and then the hours are used as and when they are needed according to the negotiated rules. But the great thing is, that if the Banked Hours are not used within the year because they were not needed, then the Banked Hours are zeroed at the end of the year. So, the shift worker will be being paid for time which they don't have to work. It is paid time off work.

If a shift worker starts off the year with 100 hours in the Bank, and they are only asked to work 40 hours of them during the year. Then the 60 hours remaining in the Bank are written off. This time off is in payment for being there, in case they were needed. However, if they were not needed then they get a bonus. They get money for nothing.

This is the main selling point of Banked Hours. **Paid time off in addition to their holidays.**

Banked Hours & Pensions

If the Banked Hours come entirely from the contracted basic hours, they will already be included in any pension arrangements. If they are additional purchased hours that are guaranteed for a limited period, they should probably be treated in the same way as overtime hours for pension purposes.

Banked Hours & Working Time Directive Holiday Entitlements

Usually, the Banked Hours will not have any impact on the number of holidays that staff are entitled to, or the holiday pay associated with the annual holiday entitlement. In the UK, the minimum holiday entitlement is 5.6 weeks. The 5.6 weeks can be regarded as being 4 weeks, or 20 days, of contracted weekly hours and 8 Bank Holidays based on the contracted week. If the Banked Hours falls entirely within the contracted hours, then no amendments need to be made. If the Banked Hours are additional hours, then again it is likely that no additional holidays are given.

Holiday pay in the UK specifies that this should reflect the average earnings over the previous 52 fully worked weeks. In other words, if the holiday entitlement is exactly 5.6 weeks, then each week of holiday should be paid at the average earnings including any Banked Hours payment. If the holiday entitlement is greater than 5.6 weeks, and it usually is, then the minimum that should be paid is 5.6 weeks of average pay. This is a fairly complicated calculation and will probably depend on an individual's holiday entitlement.

As an example, a person is paid £20,000 for 2,000 basic hours per year and is entitled to 33 days of holiday (6.6 weeks). This makes the hourly pay £10/hour. They receive 200 Banked Hours paid at +50% (£15/hour), making their total pay £23,000pa. This is £442/week and the minimum holiday payment is 5.6 times this, £2,475. As they receive 6.6 weeks of holiday pay based on the £20,000, that is £2,539 and it is more than the minimum payment. Please note that the UK Government has not decided, or illustrated, how to work out holiday pay except to say it is based on average pay over the last 52 fully worked weeks.

Calculating The Number of Banked Hours

The uses an organisation wants to put the Bank Hours to, determines the number of Banked Hours. Typical uses are; covering absences, authorised leave, training and ad-hoc work. Each of these is calculated separately.

If an organisation, using a 12-hour HISP requiring staff to work 1,800 hours per year, then a 3% absence rate equates to 54 hours of absence each on average. Thus to cover absences would require 54 hours per person in the Bank. Authorised leave, such as bereavement, paternity, etc. might be about 10 hours/year/person, training might be about 40hours/year/person and ad-hoc work might be about 24 hours/year/person. The total required, on average, is 54+10+40+24 = 128 hours/year/person.

If everything was evenly distributed through the year and a means of equally distributing the hours through the year was available, then each person would need 128 hours/year. However, absences are unlikely to fall evenly on everyone, not least because 54 hours of absence cannot be divided by 12-hour shifts. That means some staff will work on more Covers than others. Whilst over the years, this would fall equally on everyone in the long term, staff are usually very insistent that it has to be an annual event. This means that for an average of 54 hours of absence, there has to be more hours added to each person's Banked Hours to ensure that they are not exceeded in any year. This translates to having to add 25-33% extra hours for absences, taking the 54 hours to 72 hours and the annual total of Banked Hours to 146 hours/year/person.

Training is often associated with the grade of staff and the individual, for instance a new starter requires the most training. The number of hours in the Bank for each person could vary according to the grade or skill set they belong to.

Very often, absence rates include long-term sickness. However usually this is excluded from being covered by the Bank, therefore it should be deducted from the absence rate used to calculate the Banked Hours. This might have the effect of halving the absence rate, which in the above example would reduce the 54 hours to 27 hours and the 33% increase would take this to 36 hours and a total of 110 hours/person/year.

The number of Banked Hours may also be determined by the shift pattern.

Names	Hours Worked	Shifts Worked	Mon 05-Sep	Tue 06-Sep	Wed 07-Sep	Thu 08-Sep	Fri 09-Sep	Sat 10-Sep	Sun 11-Sep	Mon 12-Sep	Tue 13-Sep	Wed 14-Sep	Thu 15-Sep	Fri 16-Sep	Sat 17-Sep	Sun 18-Sep
D 07:00 21:00			3	3	3	3	3	3	3	3	3	3	3	3	3	3
C 07:00 07:00			1	1	1	1	1	1	1	1	1	1	1	1	1	1
N 21:00 07:00			3	3	3	3	3	3	3	3	3	3	3	3	3	3
Total			7	7	7	7	7	7	7	7	7	7	7	7	7	7
Team 1	2196	214	D	D	D	C			N	N	N				D	D
Team 2	2184	213	C				N	N	N			D	D	D		C
Team 3	2196	213	N	N	N				D	D	D		C		N	N
Team 4	2184	212				D	D	D		C		N	N			
Team 5	2196	214	D	D	D		C		N	N	N				D	D
Team 6	2184	213		C		N	N	N				D	D	D		
Team 7	2196	213	N	N	N				D	D	D			C	N	N
Team 8	2184	212				D	D	D		C		N	N	N		
Team 9	2196	213	D	D	D		C		N	N	N				D	D
Team 10	2184	213				C	N	N	N			D	D	D	C	
Team 11	2196	213	N	N	N				D	D	D	C			N	N
Team 12	2184	212				D	D	D	C					N	N	N

Figure 1: 3on-3off example shift pattern

Figure 1 shows an example shift pattern where 12 teams are working 12-hour shifts on the 3on-3off. At the top is the number of shifts on each day where D is a day shift 7am-7pm. C is a cover shift where they could come in to work either the day or the night shift. N is the night shift 7pm-7am.

The shift pattern gives flat staffing of three teams on 24/7. There is also one team on cover each day. So if there is an absence, someone on the cover shift could be brought in to work.

You can see that over a year everyone is working between 2,184 and 2,196 hours. This is effectively a 42 hour week.

If they were contracted to work 45 hours per week, then they would have between 150 and 162 hours in the Bank.

Using Banked Hours for Training

Training is a great use of Banked Hours. Everyone likes training, staff and unions like it because it makes them more mobile, adaptive and means that the company is investing in them. Often new equipment or techniques will be adopted, and everyone will need to be trained. Some training needs to be done regularly to ensure that people are up to date and remember key skills when called upon in an emergency. So, Fire and Health and Safety personnel will need regular training included in their shift pattern.

However, you can't always be sure when a trainer will be available, months or even years ahead. You may not even know what sort of training will be needed. Hence having a flexible approach to covering for training is necessary.

So Banked Hours is a good way to cover for training. If you expect each person to have an average amount of training, then you can ensure that the Banked Hours have enough hours available to cover for training.

Then when someone requests training, or training is required, it can be booked in on one of their days off (provided it is mutually agreeable), and they are then brought in or sent off for training. The hours that they are required to cover for the training session are taken from the Banked Hours. That way, the training does not hinder the operation in any way.

Cover shifts may be used in conjunction with the Banked Hours. If this is the case, then training could be booked in when they are scheduled to be on cover. They are then brought in on their cover shift for training instead of absence cover. Very simple and convenient.

If they are on shift when the trainer is available, then you can cover their shift with the person scheduled to cover and change their shift to a training shift. Just as simple.

Banked Hours means that you can ensure that everyone is fully trained.

Not everyone will require the same amount of training. New starters may require more training, or, more intricate skills may require regular refresher courses. Banked Hours means that everyone can have a different amount of training built in to their

Banked Hours to ensure that they have enough hours to cover their training requirement.

Many complex jobs need refresher days after a person has been absent for two weeks or more. Technology based organisations or operations with regular changes need people to be brought up to date after they have been away for extended periods. On a holidays included shift pattern these extended breaks happen regularly. So on their first day back at work they may come in an hour earlier, to be updated on recent developments. Or even come in the day prior to their first shift and have a refresher course on their duties. The length of the day should reflect the amount of work required to be covered, not their standard shift length. So, they may come in for a 6-hour day before their first shift back, because that is considered the correct length of time required.

Skills Matrix

Often operations require multiple skills. For example, let's consider a call centre which works in five languages. If everyone only knows one language, then each person can only cover for absent colleagues in their own language. However, if everyone knows two languages then everyone can cover for everyone else if there is enough, planned, overlap.

Skills Matrix Table

A skills matrix is a table that shows you who has which skills.

Let's consider the five languages example. We will start with just five skills and six people to make the operation simple. So on shift we need five people and one person is cover. Let's have each person being responsible for a primary language and also being able to converse in a secondary language. In the matrix the primary language will be shown with an "X", and "Y" shows their secondary language.

Table 1: Example Skills Matrix with common language

	English	French	Spanish	German	Italian
Tom	X	Y			
Sahih	Y	X			
Jean	Y		X		
Helena	Y			X	
Jack	Y				X
Cieza	Y		X		

In table 1, this skills matrix example has everyone being able to converse in one common language, English.

Now in the first example everyone has two skills. And everyone has a common language (which would make running the operation easier). However not everyone can cover for everyone else. Six people have the ability to converse in English. Therefore, regardless of any absence, the English jobs can be covered, as there will always be someone there who can speak English. There are two people who can speak French. So, provided Tom or Sahih is in, then the French jobs can be covered as they can both speak French. Jean and Cieza can both speak Spanish, so provided one of them is there, then the Spanish jobs can be covered. Helena is the only one who can speak German and Jack is the only one to speak Italian. Therefore, if either of them are absent, there is no one to cover their German or Italian work.

What is needed, is that every skill, or language in this example, has at least two people who are proficient.

Table 2: Example Skills Matrix with two people per language

	English	French	Spanish	German	Italian
Tom	X	Y			
Sahih	Y	X			
Jean			X	Y	
Helena			Y	X	
Jack				Y	X
Cieza			X		Y

In table 2, this skills matrix example shows that every language has two people who are proficient.

Now in the second example everyone has two skills. However, there is no common language (either the manager can converse with everyone or they all speak a different common language). Now every language has at least two people who can cover the work. However not everyone can cover for everyone else. Tom and Sahih can both cover English and French. However, no one else can cover for them. So, if either is absent, then the remaining person can cover either English or French, but not both at the same time.

This time there is lots of cover for Spanish, German and Italian. You have four people, covering three languages, and each language has at least two people who can cover the work. Therefore, if Jean is absent, then Cieza can cover Spanish and Helena will cover German and Jack will cover Italian. If Helena is absent, then Jack still covers Italian and Jean and Cieza cover for Spanish and German. If Jack is absent, then Cieza covers Italian and Jean and Helena cover for Spanish and German. If Cieza is absent, then Jean covers Spanish, Helena covers German and Jack covers Italian.

If Jack's second skill was in French instead of German, then everyone can cover for everyone else.

Table 3: Example Skills Matrix with complete cover

	English	French	Spanish	German	Italian
Tom	X	Y			
Sahih	Y	X			
Jean			X	Y	
Helena			Y	X	
Jack		Y			X
Cieza			X		Y

Table 3 shows an example skills matrix where there is cover for all languages. Therefore, if one person is absent, then all of the languages can still be covered.

Now in the third example everyone has two skills as before. However, again there is no common language, but everyone can cover for any of the other five, so they can all converse provided they all translate for each other. Now every language has at least two people who can cover the work. Also, no group is isolated.

So, if Tom is absent, then Sahih covers English, Jack covers French, Jean covers Spanish, Helena covers German and Cieza covers Italian. If Sahih is absent, then Tom covers English, Jack covers French, Jean covers Spanish, Helena covers German and Cieza covers Italian. If Jean is absent, then Tom covers English, Sahih covers French, Cieza covers Spanish, Helena covers German and Jack covers Italian. If Helena is absent, then Tom covers English, Sahih covers French, Cieza covers Spanish, Jean covers German and Jack covers Italian. If Jack is absent, then Tom covers English, Sahih covers French, Jean covers Spanish, Helena covers German and Cieza covers Italian. If Cieza is absent, then Tom covers English, Sahih covers French, Jean covers Spanish, Helena covers German and Jack covers Italian.

The cost of having one person on cover to cover five skills is much less than having five additional people to cover the five skills. There is an initial cost in training staff, but the motto here is **"train them once, but use them often"**. A one-off training cost compared to having four extra staff on permanent cover is an excellent investment.

The Skills Matrix is a simple way to look up who can cover for whom. It can be as large and as complicated as you need. For a large operation, it is not unheard of to have fifty skills being required and hundreds of people in the matrix. Power companies regularly use skills matrix. Our local PowerStation has a skills matrix with 42 skills. A food producer can have dozens of skills: warehouse input, mixing, oven, freezer, packaging, labelling, IT, QC, Team Leader, sales and planners. With a different skill for each production line.

To make up your own skills matrix simply make a list of every job. Start with one operation or department. Some of the jobs will be very similar, and so you can combine these jobs under one skill set. Some jobs may require a level of technical knowledge and others may just require basic training. You need to group the different levels of skills.

Once you have a list of all the skills, you can then create a matrix. Note down the skills across the top and the list of people employed in the area/department. Then mark down what skills they have. "X" for a primary skill, "Y" to indicate a secondary skill which they can cover.

You can then check to make sure that you have enough people and skills distribution to cover for absences. You can also use it to assess what skills are missing and use it for recruitment. The degree of skills might be a factor, so when deciding who to train, you can choose people depending on the level of expertise they already have.

A skills matrix is a very useful tool for managing and maintaining operations.

Stepping up/Stepping down

All companies need their employees to step up or step down. A manager is the typical example. If someone is absent and the manager can't find someone to cover, then the manager needs to step down to that role. This has its own problems if the manager can't do two jobs at once, they can't cover for the absent person and do their own work. Hence the operation is less efficient, and work needs to be passed on to the next shift or delayed till the manager is back on duty. What's more the company is paying a manager to do the work of a lower skilled employee.

That being said, you do need the flexibility. Allowing people to stepdown is essential for many companies to cover for absent colleagues.

Stepping up is also an essential part of any operation. All operations need some form of management and if the manager is ill or on holiday, then their necessary day to day activities need to be covered by someone else. So, the assistant manager or a senior supervisor may step-up.

When someone changes role for a shift, they do not need to do everything that is required of that role. They only need to do as much as is needed to get through the shift. However, it is often useful for people to do other roles. When it comes to promotions it is useful for the person to have stepped up in the past. That way they know what at least part of the role consists of and the review board can see how they have performed.

Regular rotation of skills is often essential in keeping those skills current. Hence many companies build in a skills rotation into the shift pattern. So, every month or three months people have to work in their secondary skill to ensure that they are up to date.

Stepping up or down fits in well with Banked Hours. Different groups or skill sets may work different hours. For example, if you have three groups of staff each with different skills, you may well employ more of one set than needed and use them as absence cover. This could come out naturally or be intentional. If it is the lowest skill, then it may be cheaper. However, employees will then have to regularly step up. This regular stepping up could come with a payment or be a necessity for promotions. You can predict how often it will happen each year and then only give payments if it is over the estimate, the regular stepping up is then just part of the job and already covered in their pay. You could also use the Banked hour as a way of paying for stepping up. For example, if they step up, then one Banked Hours is taken off their Bank, as an acknowledgment of the increase in responsibility.

Alternatively, it could be the highest skill which has the larger Bank and covers for absence. This way the company pays more but are assured that the person covering will be able to do the work well.

The people who cover, could also be a group of volunteers. They could be recruited from all of the skill sets and step up or step down as and when needed.

Banked Hours and Training

Everyone likes training. Training means that the company is investing in them as an individual. The more training, they have, the more valuable they become. Banked Hours is a great way to ensure that everyone receives the correct training.

With Banked Hours you can bring people in on their day off for training and not worry about the cost of overtime etc. the training time is budgeted for in the Banked Hours system. So, when a training opportunity comes along, the individual or their manager can arrange it without worrying about how it will affect the operation. The individuals could, if allowed, arrange their course themselves on your Banked Hours.

Without the Banked Hours system, people need to be released from their duties to go off on training. However, with the Banked Hours system, there is a backup person available if they are down to work on the training day or they can be brought in on their day off.

So Banked Hours means that they can have the training they need to improve and stay current without putting the work or their colleagues at risk.

Covering for Absences

Absences are stressful for everyone.

The absent person feels they are letting down their team. "How will they cope without me?" they wonder.

The manager has to contact people outside of working time and beg them to come in to work and cover. If they can't get anyone to come in and cover they are left with the choice of covering the absence themselves (not a great way to spend your Saturday night) or reorganise the operation so that they can still do something when running short.

The other shift workers are harassed by the manager, begging them to come in to work on their day off. If they give in, yes it means extra money, but they are then working in a strange environment with other people. The other people working on shift resent them because they are being paid more to do the same job and not doing it as well because they don't know how this team works.

The team mates have to cope with either some useless person from another team coming in, or they have their manager stepping down to work with them, and who likes that, or they are all forced to work harder just because *so and so* has the gall to become ill.

All in all, it is not a pleasant experience for anyone. And it happens daily.

Whereas on a Banked Hours system there is no stress. The absence person can relax and get better knowing that there is a system in place. Their team will cope just fine without them as they will know exactly who will come in and cover. So, they can focus all of their energy on getting well.

The manager no longer has to beg anyone. They merely consult the rota and inform the person who is due to come in and cover, when they are required. There is no rearranging of schedules. They no longer have to worry about whether they can meet their deadlines. They know they can meet them.

The other shift workers are not disturbed at home. They are informed when they are needed on their cover day and will only be asked to work on these pre-arranged dates. When they do come in, with a lot of notice, they are no longer the odd one out. They will have the necessary skills and they will have worked with everyone regularly, so they know what they have to do and the operation runs smoothly.

The team mates welcome the replacement, because they know they will be working with them regularly. It is merely part and parcel of the operation. They don't have to worry that they will be asked to work harder because someone is absent. They know they never will.

Banked Hours is about reducing stress and ensuring that everyone enjoys the benefits of a smooth operation.

Absence and Sickness

Absence is the largest unplanned expense organisations face daily.

We cannot avoid absences and they are very distracting to managers. They use a disproportionate amount of management time and managers often fail in covering them if an informal cover plan is used, irrespective of the effort involved.

The use of a formal cover arrangement carries a cost, but the income generated by maintaining operations is much higher.

In an 'office hours' operation or a 2-shift system, you can't have the staff covering for each other because everyone is working every day anyway. The way most companies operate is to either replace the person using agency staff or move an internal person off their job onto the absentee's job. If you do not cover the absence, you lose the income the absentee generates.

You might be able to catch up with the work by using overtime after normal operating hours, because there is no one else internally you can call on. You might be able to use a coping strategy, such as coping without the person, rearranging the work, deferring work to another time, or closing down the operation.

But wouldn't it be better to bring in a fully trained person familiar with all aspects of the operation, which is exactly what you can do when you have shift working, although for the 2 shift system it may include operating 16-hour shifts.

8-hour shifts can usually be converted to 12-hour shifts to cater for an absence and shift patterns using 12-hour shifts always have some staff not at work every day of the week.

The reason why organisations have cover arrangements by shift workers for absent shift workers is – **because they can**.

The Primary Principles

Absences can only be covered by staff with a similar skill; such as Operators can only cover Operators or Engineers can only cover Engineers. That is part of their responsibility.

The following are not options that an organisation would normally use:

- Premises left uncovered or Equipment insufficiently staffed
- Doubling up staffing on all shifts in all skills
- Contract workers
- Managers or Supervisors replacing absent staff

Therefore an organisation needs another solution.

Cover Strategies

There are three common cover strategies:

1. Cover by staff already scheduled to work on the day
2. Cover by staff scheduled off for the day
3. Coping by managers

Cover Arrangements

There are four parts to consider in Absence Cover Arrangements;

- Reward Structure
- Notification Time
- Rest Time
- De-motivators

Reward Structure

The reward structure has two main categories:

1. Payment

The payment arrangements fall into two categories:

- Payments in Advance
- Payments if staff work.

2. Time Off In Lieu (TOIL)

Sometimes the TOIL is at enhanced rates, i.e. 1.5 days off for each day of work.

And, the occasional "thank you" from the 'boss'.

Notification of Working When on Cover

Notification falls into two time periods:

1. Long term notification, of shifts, or part shifts, to be covered by individuals. Often this is classified as greater than 24-hours' notice.
2. Short Term Notification of actual work required by an individual and duration of work period. This means bringing in staff with as little as zero notice but usually much more, and not necessarily for whole shifts. This depends on the Coping Strategy set up by Management.

Rest Time

Rest falls into two categories:

- Rest prior to cover period if work is required.
- Rest after period of work.

Legal Obligations

This falls into two parts:

- Obligations to the staff by the company.
- Obligations to the company by the staff.

De-motivators

People think that cover systems are unfair. They feel "put upon". "Why me?" they ask. They do not see the big picture. They don't know what is going on. All they see is that it is Saturday night and instead of going down the pub or enjoying a night at home with the family, you have called them up, again, and asked them to come into work.

That is unless you are paying them an exorbitant amount of money. Then the unfairness shifts, from "why is it always me?", to "why is it never me?"

So regardless of which case you have, your biggest problem will be unfairness. **Share out the pleasure, share out the pain!**

Then there is the issue of the person who was not expecting to work. They are insufficiently rested. Their family or friends are now disrupted by their absence. They must be sober, contactable, and be ready to go into work at a moment's notice. They need to arrange transport to get into work. And then they are expected to perform expertly in a strange location with unknown colleagues, after they have delayed the handover by having their "job for the day" discussed with them.

If after having this alien situation forced on them, they make a mistake, then they are obviously at fault and face disciplinary action.

If they decline the "invitation" to come in, what happens? Will they never be asked to work overtime again? Will they face disciplinary action? Will they not be promoted?

Perhaps not all the above applies in every instance, but that is how staff often look at it. In general, it puts the staff 'on the spot'.

When on-call is brought up, people's biggest fear is that they are always on-call. They are never off duty. An on-call rota is the only fair and viable solution. It is the only way to ensure that people are not brought in when they are not expecting to come in.

An on-call rota is the only way to guarantee that everyone has an equal chance at overtime, or an equal chance of having their Saturday night interrupted.

Cover Policy Instigator

If you set up a Cover Policy and a Cover Arrangement, you also need to decide who is responsible for activating it at the time it is required, and this may be late on a Saturday for instance. The best policy, but rarely happens, is for the Supervisor in charge of the shift to make this decision. That is because they would know the most appropriate course of action for their shift.

However, if you want to bring in a replacement, you can't wait till after the shift has started. By then it will be too late to bring someone in. So you can appreciate that decisions have to be made as early as possible. Waiting for the shift to start before making a decision is not the best policy.

Therefore, a Supervisor on one shift often has to make a decision about the next shift. Invariably, the 'safest' course of action is taken, and the Cover Arrangement is activated, whether it is actually needed or not.

Coping Strategy

A Coping Strategy determines the actions to be taken in the event of an absence. For sickness at short notice, under 24 hours, a typical strategy would ask the following questions to determine the appropriate action:

- Can we cope without the absentee?
- Can we move the work to another time?
- Can we close the operation?
- Can we reorganize the staff to cover the absence?
- Can we ask staff to go home later and/or come to work earlier?
- Can we call in another person to work the shift?

Very often the last question on the list is the first response to this problem. If the other questions are answered first, in the negative, then the staff that are brought in understand that there is no other solution.

For Sickness with a longer notice, you can make another decision. The more time you have to plan, the better the outcome will be.

Making the decision before the event happens and then having a policy in place means, that the best solution will always be implemented. So it is worth sitting down with all of the interested parties and devising plans and contingencies. Then everyone knows what will happen and the solution can be implemented seamlessly.

What Happens in Practice

Most of the time, because the amount of time set aside is more than is usually needed, the staff would not use all of the hours in the Bank. At the end of each year, the unused Banked Hours are saved for use in future years, or the unused hours are given to the staff and the Bank is zeroed. Most unions will insist that the Bank is Zeroed or only a limited amount of hours can be carried over into the following year.

The time allotted to the Bank is usually based on the maximum expected usage by looking back over several years and evaluating how much time would have been required in each year. Sometimes, there are very rare events that might cause this number to be extremely high, or, there may have been hardly any absences and no training requirements over the last few years. This means that a 'common sense' appraisal is made of the previous years of data to ensure that all parties are in agreement on what should be the right number of hours in the Bank.

Often, it is thought that the Banked Hours system is self-policing and a way of reducing absences when it comes to sickness as it requires staff to provide cover for each other. Whilst this system does deter staff from reporting in sick for mild causes, it should be emphasised that the company does not want seriously ill staff to come to work, just because it causes inconveniences to other staff. It is a case of striking a balance between deterrence and inconvenience.

Peer Pressures

The Banked Hours system is activated when a person is absent. As no further payments are made if a person is called in to work, then each person on-call will gain nothing by working that extra shift. Thus they are inconvenienced. If they feel this was not necessary as the cause of the absence was not a severe illness, they are likely to express their feelings to the cause of their inconvenience. This imposes a duty onto their fellow workers; to report in absences at the earliest possible moment and restrict the absence to the minimum possible.

Often the absent person will phone the on-call person and arrange a shift-swap to avoid an absence at all. The person being absent knows that someone will be working in their place, but if they swap their shift with that person, who will work it anyway, and have a reverse swap for some time in the future, both staff are helping each other. It is not unknown for absences to drop to zero.

Fairness Criteria

Often, the staff would like to set up a fairness criteria, this is to ensure that staff are equally used and equally inconvenienced. There are three factors to consider when setting up any fairness criteria. The first is that the staff will very often start the year with different number of hours in the Bank. This is because it is very hard to equal out all of the hours over a year and often staff will have different amounts of holiday entitlement. Therefore, staff would like to all work the same number of hours at the end of the year. This has to be balanced with both the on-call set up for arranging cover, and for the actual incidents that cause staff to come into work.

In general, this problem falls into two categories, the on-call roster and the number of occasions of actually working a shift. Staff find that they are far more often on-call than the number of times they actually work. This means they would like a system which puts all staff equally on-call. However, initially, the focus is on the number of occasions that they might work whilst on-call and that the number of shifts worked is equalised. For a company, as long as the cover is provided, the method of ensuring that cover and the setting up of a Fairness Criteria is often delegated to the staff, or their representative committee.

In practice the two categories are incompatible, and the decision has to be about, which category takes precedence? The on-call roster, or the worked shifts. For instance, if one person (A) works more shifts on Banked Hours than another, (B), in the past few months, then to equalise the worked shifts in the future few months, they need to alter the on-call roster to put (A) on fewer on-call sessions than (B), who should be on more on-call sessions and therefore more likely to be called in to work a shift. This means that the on-call roster has to be reset every few months. However, (B) might feel that more on-call sessions is just as unfair as actually working, and so the Fairness Criteria would need to equate the number of on-call sessions and the number of worked shifts to a formula.

Usually, it is eventually recognised that it is not easy to set up a Fairness Criteria that everyone regards as fair, and the end result is that the committee decides that Fate is the best system, and if one person works more shifts in one period, Fate will probably cause them to work fewer shifts in the next period of time. However, this needs to be evolved by the staff representatives to ensure that all staff are involved in the final decisions.

Terms of Employment Clause Example

The shift pattern will provide the means by which staff will work their Contracted Hours. In the event that not all the Contracted Hours are included in the shift pattern, then all remaining hours will provide a Bank of Hours to be used for other purposes.

The Bank of Hours will be required for the following:

Sickness absence cover including elective surgery

Authorised Leave (Bereavement, etc.)

Training days

Ad-hoc workloads

Force majeure events

Contingency for unforeseen and unplannable events

Leavers

All unused Banked Hours will be discarded at the end of each year.

A Fairness Criteria will be applied to the Banked Hours on an annual basis.

In the case of Banked Hours, less is more. The more they are defined, the less flexible they become.

Computer Model

The easiest way to run a Banked Hours system is via a computer model accessible to managers, rather than a paper system or a Time & Attendance system. A computer model can produce a visual display of the Banked Hours and can be easily accessed by staff to ascertain if the system is fair or biased. Running a Banked Hours system only takes a few minutes each day. As the changes to the shift pattern are made, the Bank automatically changes up or down. The model can include a 'traffic light system' to show if it is running as predicted, or not.

The best software is VisualrotaX, which has been specially designed to run a Banked hours system. VisualrotaX allows you to create the shift pattern on a yearly basis, and then does all the calculations for you. Therefore, on any given day you can see at a glance, how many Banked Hours are available, and who owes them. Any changes to the shift pattern will result in the calculations being automatically updated.

Banked Hours and Cover Shifts

Banked Hours go hand in hand with cover shifts. In fact, if you try to run a Banked Hours system without cover shifts, you will run into problems. The issue is, how do you get people to come in on a day off when you have already paid for those hours?

This is where cover shifts come in. It makes life easier for everyone. So, cover shifts are not really shifts. They are a designated day when you can ask someone to come in. They may be a designated shift, e.g. day cover and night cover. Or they could be just a designated date, and you can ask a person to come in on any shift.

Let's take the 12-hour 232 shift pattern. The 232 is great for demonstrating the cover shifts because it has some unique features. Here we shall have the 232 with 25 people on holidays included. There are five employees scheduled on every shift. On this pattern there are going to be two people on each day for "Cover". They are to be numbered C1 and C2. There are 365 days per year, therefore there are 730 cover shifts per year. Therefore, in an average year each person would be down to cover about 30 days. 15 of which will be the C1 shifts and 15 will be the C2 shifts.

Figure 2 shows how the shift pattern would look in practice. There are 25 people on the 232 holidays included shift pattern. Therefore, each day five people are scheduled to work. There are also two people down each day for cover. These cover shifts are designated by C1 and C2. The cover shifts in this example are to be worked between the day and the night shifts. This way they do not interrupt the long breaks. Also the cover shifts are joined on after the day shifts or before the night shifts. This way no one is working a single shift. They can cover either the day or the night shift without impinging on the shifts on either side. Also the weekend cover shifts are together. This minimises the disruption to the weekends and no one will work more than four consecutive shifts.

Figure 2: 232 shift pattern for 25 people with cover shifts

232			01 January 2020 - 30 December 2020																			
	Start Time	Finish Time	Wednesday	Thursday	Friday	Saturday	Sunday	Monday	Tuesday	Wednesday	Thursday	Friday	Saturday	Sunday	Monday	Tuesday	Wednesday	Thursday	Friday	Saturday	Sunday	Monday
D	07:00	19:00	5	5	5	5	5	5	5	5	5	5	5	5	5	5	5	5	5	5	5	5
N	19:00	07:00	5	5	5	5	5	5	5	5	5	5	5	5	5	5	5	5	5	5	5	5
C1	07:00	07:00	1	1	1	1	1	1	1	1	1	1	1	1	1	1	1	1	1	1	1	1
C2	07:00	07:00	1	1	1	1	1	1	1	1	1	1	1	1	1	1	1	1	1	1	1	1
Total			12	12	12	12	12	12	12	12	12	12	12	12	12	12	12	12	12	12	12	12
P1	1690.5	178	C1		N	N	N			D	D		C2	C2	N	N			D	D	D	
P2	1690.5	176		C1	N	N	N			D	D				N	N			D	D	D	C2
P3	1690.5	177	C2		N	N	N			D	D	C1			N	N			D	D	D	
P4	1690.5	178		C2	N	N	N			D	D		C1	C1	N	N			D	D	D	
P5	1690.5	176			N	N	N			D	D	C2			N	N			D	D	D	C1
P6	1702	179	D	D		C2	C2	N	N			D	D	D		C1	N	N				
P7	1702	177	D	D				N	N			D	D	D	C2		N	N				
P8	1702	178	D	D	C1			N	N			D	D	D		C2	N	N				
P9	1702	178	D	D		C1	C1	N	N			D	D	D			N	N				
P10	1702	178	D	D	C2			N	N			D	D	D	C1		N	N				
P11	1667.5	174			D	D	D		C1	N	N											D
P12	1667.5	174			D	D	D	C2		N	N											D
P13	1667.5	174			D	D	D		C2	N	N											D
P14	1667.5	173			D	D	D			N	N											D
P15	1667.5	174			D	D	D	C1		N	N											D
P16	1656	172	N	N											D	D		C1	N	N	N	
P17	1656	173	N	N											D	D	C2		N	N	N	
P18	1656	172	N	N											D	D		C2	N	N	N	
P19	1656	172	N	N											D	D			N	N	N	
P20	1656	173	N	N											D	D	C1		N	N	N	
P21	1679	175						D	D		C1	N	N	N			D	D				N
P22	1679	175						D	D	C2		N	N	N			D	D	C1			N
P23	1679	175						D	D		C2	N	N	N			D	D		C1	C1	N
P24	1679	174						D	D			N	N	N			D	D	C2			N
P25	1679	175						D	D	C1		N	N	N			D	D		C2	C2	N

		CDT											Example							
	Tuesday	Wednesday	Thursday	Friday	Saturday	Sunday	Monday	Tuesday	Wednesday	Thursday	Friday	Saturday	Sunday	Monday	Tuesday	Wednesday	Thursday	Friday	Saturday	Sunday
D	5	5	5	5	5	5	5	5	5	5	5	5	5	5	5	5	5	5	5	5
N	5	5	5	5	5	5	5	5	5	5	5	5	5	5	5	5	5	5	5	5
C1	1	1	1	1	1	1	1	1	1	1	1	1	1	1	1	1	1	1	1	1
C2	1	1	1	1	1	1	1	1	1	1	1	1	1	1	1	1	1	1	1	1
Total	12	12	12	12	12	12	12	12	12	12	12	12	12	12	12	12	12	12	12	12
P1	C1	N	N											D	D		C1	N	N	N
P2		N	N											D	D	C2		N	N	N
P3	C2	N	N											D	D		C2	N	N	N
P4		N	N											D	D			N	N	N
P5		N	N											D	D	C1		N	N	N
P6							D	D		C1	N	N	N			D	D			
P7							D	D	C2		N	N	N			D	D	C1		
P8							D	D		C2	N	N	N			D	D		C1	C1
P9							D	D			N	N	N			D	D	C2		
P10							D	D	C1		N	N	N			D	D		C2	C2
P11	D		C1	N	N	N			D	D				N	N			D	D	D
P12	D	C2		N	N	N			D	D	C1			N	N			D	D	D
P13	D		C2	N	N	N			D	D		C1	C1	N	N			D	D	D
P14	D			N	N	N			D	D	C2			N	N			D	D	D
P15	D	C1		N	N	N			D	D		C2	C2	N	N			D	D	D
P16		D	D				N	N			D	D	D	C2		N	N			
P17		D	D	C1			N	N			D	D	D		C2	N	N			
P18		D	D		C1	C1	N	N			D	D	D			N	N			
P19		D	D	C2			N	N			D	D	D	C1		N	N			
P20		D	D		C2	C2	N	N			D	D	D		C1	N	N			
P21	N			D	D	D	C2		N	N										
P22	N			D	D	D		C2	N	N										
P23	N			D	D	D			N	N										
P24	N			D	D	D	C1		N	N										
P25	N			D	D	D		C1	N	N										

If they are on the C1 shifts, then they will be the first one called in to cover for an absence. If they are the C2 shifts, then they will cover the second absence. If there are more than two absences on any day, the cover shift will not be used to cover the third absence. That will need to be covered by overtime, running short, moving the work or having the manager step down.

The cover shifts have no hours associated with them. Each team is down to work a slightly different number of shifts, this is because the shift pattern has a five-week rotation (not including the cover shifts). The year is 52.14 weeks, therefore they are midway through a cycle at the end of the year.

In this example, the shifts are 11.5 hours (paid) long. So, the scheduled hours for the year vary between 1,656 and 1,702 hours. You can see the number of hours they would each be scheduled to work in the second column in figure 2. Now if the contract was set at 39-hours per week, and they had 6 weeks of holiday per year, each person should be down to work 1,794 hours per year after holidays, (if a year was taken to 52 weeks). Hence each team would have a different number of Banked Hours.

Team 1 would each have 103.5 Banked Hours (1794-1690.5=103.5). Team 2 would have 92 Banked Hours. Team 3 would have 126.5 Banked Hours. Team 4 would have 138 Banked Hours. Team 5 would have 115 Banked Hours.

This means that the group as a whole would have 2,875 Banked Hours. This could cover for five days of training each and an absence rate of about 3%. If no one was absent and no training took place, it is an extra three weeks off a year that they would be working.

Work/life Balance

The cover shifts in the 232 example are there to improve the shift workers work/life balance. The cover shifts are put into the natural gaps in the pattern outside of the shift workers' long breaks. This way it doesn't disrupt their long breaks. On this shift pattern, they would have about 10 lots of 10-days off, or eight lots of 10-day breaks and a 17-day break in the summer depending on how the shift pattern was designed.

The shifts themselves are grouped into clusters of two or three shifts, with two or three days off in-between. This helps minimise fatigue on shift. The shift pattern works around the week so that they are either working or not working the weekend. This shift pattern is one of the most popular shift patterns.

There are two places where the cover shifts can be entered. Either between the day and night shifts as shown in figure 2, or in their long breaks. If they were in their long breaks, they would need to lose about five of their long breaks. So, it would probably be more popular to fit them in around the shifts and leave their long breaks sacrosanct.

The cover shifts are all about improving the shift workers lives. If they don't have them, then each day they are off, they are in danger of being called in to work their Banked Hours. With the Cover shifts, this is no longer the case. They are down to cover about 30 days per year. On these days, they are expected to be ready to come in if needed. This means that on their days off, (186-194 days off in the year), they are not subject to the company requiring that they come into work. So, for over half the year, their days off, are theirs. They can do what they want, go on holiday or stay home, free from the stress or worry that they may need to come into work, just because someone is absent.

If they are requested to come in, then they must come in. Failure to do so is subject to the same disciplinary action as being absent on shift. Some companies allow one or two refusals in a year. Others release employees from being on-call as soon as everyone is at work on the shift. Some keep an employee at work until the replacement has arrived.

This system means that their work/life balance is improved from the standard call in or running short. Now no one needs to worry about being absent. They are not putting undue strain on their colleagues. There is a system in place and they can relax. The managers can also relax. If someone is absent, then they no longer have to call up everyone and ask them to come in. They just make one phone call. The person on the C1 shift will know they have to come in, so there is no pleading. The manager merely informs them when they need to come in. The Banked Hours system means that the payment is already dealt with and within the budget. If there is a second absence, then the C2 person is called.

It makes covering for absence simple and effective.

The system is also fair. Everyone is rotated equally through the shift pattern and the cover shifts. They all work C1 and C2 shifts in an almost equal manner over the year (365 days is very awkward).

There is no favoritism. The shift pattern selects who is to come in, not a person or manager. Some years people will be lucky. Other years they will be unlucky. However, they will always oscillate around the mean.

Typical questions from employees centre around being contacted and what happens if they are ill when on-call. These questions are discussed, negotiated and become the rules of operation. Employees often view Banked Hours as impinging on their freedom of action on their days off, rather than bring up all the benefits of having a fully skilled shift to work with. The benefits to the employees far outweigh any imposition made by using Banked Hours.

Few questions are ever asked about why employees are not brought in to make their work easier when an absence occurs. In this respect, managers and employees are in accord, they want the work to be easy for everyone.

In the example above with 5 people on a shift, if one person is off sick, four people would be inconvenienced by the absence if no one was available. If one person is on-call and called in, then only one person is inconvenienced.

In the above example each person is on Cover about 30 times during the year. If they weren't using a Banked Hours arrangement, then they would need to be at work on 10 extra shifts to make up their contracted and paid for hours. For 25 employees that is about 250 shifts, or about 5 shifts per week. A company would still need absence cover and so they would roster in these shifts on the most vulnerable shifts, namely the weekend shifts, especially the weekend night shifts. So it could mean each person working 5 more weekends, or 10 extra Night shifts. By having an on-call cover arrangement, they don't need to be on shift. Training is never at night nor on weekends, and a 3% absence rate would mean that on the 52 Saturday Night shifts with the extra person, there will be about 8 absences. This means that the cover arrangement allows 44 people to have the Saturday Night off which they would otherwise have to work. If they do work it on the cover arrangement because of an absence, it will be about once in three years. Definitely seems like a win-win.

Uses of Banked Hours

There are very few restrictions on the uses of the Banked Hours as long as they are used for the Primary purpose of ensuring continuity of Operations. Whatever is necessary to give an organisation continuity of operations, working with the correct number of staff with the correct skills on each shift, is covered by the Banked Hours. After all, that is the purpose of the Bank, since if the Operation could run without the absent staff on duty, there would be no need for the Bank and all the staff would be rostered to work just their contracted hours per week, that is, they would work on more days in the year

The secondary purpose of the Banked Hours is to minimise the disruption to the staff by providing the cover in a controlled and rostered manner. Thus the staff will know when they might be needed and when they definitely won't be needed.

Part of any Operational requirement is Training, and these are often included in Banked Hours because Training is difficult to plan far in advance. Training time, and similar activities such as meetings, is often by mutual arrangements between the staff and managers and will always be planned in advance.

Legal leave (jury duty, etc.) and company approved Leave (compassionate, etc.) is also covered by Banked Hours if there are no other means of providing cover.

Leavers would often cause shifts to be short staffed if a replacement cannot be employed and trained in time to cause a seamless transfer of shifts without the Banked Hours.

Most causes of using the Banked Hours can be determined in frequency and duration by examining the events in the last few years. This sets the bandwidth of events in the future. It is inappropriate to calculate the number of Banked Hours required by speculating on possible combinations of rare events, and extrapolating to deduce that these will happen every year.

Holidays will often be included within the shift pattern, whether HISP or HESP, then the most likely events that cause the Bank Hours to be used will be Training and sickness absence. Special leaves and long illnesses are, by their nature, rare events. All companies should plan to replace staff as they retire, or leave, ahead of the event, but external factors might affect the actual timing of these events occurring seamlessly. The Banked Hours would then play an important part in ensuring the continuity of Operations.

Cover Roster

For 12-hour shifts, the cover has to be provided by staff not scheduled to work on the shift being covered. The cover arrangements are set up as a schedule of shifts that each individual is assigned to cover. This means that on days that a person is not working or down to cover, they are not going to be required to work. This roster can be set up for as long in advance as desired, and typically this is a year ahead.

It is usual for the staff to arrange the roster details in collaboration with management.

Leavers and Retirees

This topic is always discussed. Perhaps the biggest fear of the staff is that any remaining hours in the Bank will be used to cover for Leavers, indefinitely. Thus, recruiting is delayed, because it can be delayed. Also, that the Bank is used to cover the training period of new starters. Their fear is that these are deliberate management policies to exploit the Cover system. They will probably ask that Leavers are not part of the arrangements, which is not a practical option usually.

A mid-way position is to arrange for cover for Leavers to have a time limit, after which other means will be used. With hundreds of shift workers in an organisation, then in every year there will be many Leavers so they cannot realistically be excluded from the Banked Hours scheme.

Retirees are a different class of leaver as their date of leaving is known well in advance and would probably be excluded from the scheme.

Questions that may come up are:

- What happens if a Leaver, on their date of leaving still has many hours in their Bank?
- Should the company deduct these hours from their final payment or let them go?
- Or use them up by demanding extra shifts be worked?

Every company has a different policy on this, so there isn't a consensual opinion on the best course of action. Some companies deduct the hours by calculating how many hours should have been worked compared with the actual hours worked. This is often counterproductive as the Leaver leaves at little or no notice at the most inconvenient time with insufficient monies outstanding to make the deduction. Other companies take the philosophical approach that the Leaver has helped guarantee Operations during their time, they will give a reasonable notice of leaving, and the company ignores any remaining hours in the Bank. A catch-all phrase can be 'at Manager's discretion'.

HISP & Leavers

The previous section deals with Bank Hours and Leavers. Most companies using a HESP have a clause in their Terms of Employment stating that they will pay for or deduct monies for, unused holidays or too many holidays taken. The clause is still valid in a HISP but is difficult, in practice, to apply. It requires an enormous amount of paperwork, records and many calculations to perform an exact calculation of the final payment to a Leaver. It is not the best method to use, is rarely correct, and the Leaver does not have a clue if it is correct, causing an under or over payment. There is a far better method, easily calculated and cost-neutral to the company.

This method is to have the date of leaving set the final payment on a pro-rata basis. Thus a person leaving at the end of a pay period receives 100% of their usual pay, or if they leave on the 14th day of a 30-day month pay period they receive 14/30ths of their usual pay. This is irrespective of their actual hours worked. This topic will be raised at some point by the staff.

Other Flexibility Controls

The Banked Hours system can run in tandem with most other systems of flexing hours and shifts. This gives the ability to schedule occasional hours as well as shifts. It also allows hours to move in and out of the Bank.

For example: Floating Days or Golden Days (holidays additional to those included in a HISP) can be covered by Banked Hours. Thus, when a Floating Day is requested, a replacement mechanism must be in place if we are not to go back to a position where a manager has to phone around for replacement staff working on overtime rates. Certain constraints can also be imposed, such that a Floating Day from Friday Night to Sunday

Night cannot be allowed unless the requestor provides the replacement who may decide that the time comes from his Bank of hours. In this situation, the more logical approach would be to arrange a shift swap instead.

Another example: if a person has used his Floating Days (if you have agreed to have them in the system, of course) then the Bank can provide a means of having extra days off. He (or she) can arrange for another person to work the shift and this person would use his Banked Hours. The person having the Day Off puts those hours into the Bank and increases their Bank. This has a neutral effect on the Bank as a whole, so it can be permitted. This can be repeated by the second person on several other occasions until he has no more Bank hours left.

Why would he do this? There are two possible reasons. Firstly, he has arranged his working hours down to the last shift, so he knows exactly what he will be working for the next year, which may be worth more to him than the 'possibility' that he will get the remaining Bank Hours written off at the end of the year. Stability might be worth the cost. Or secondly, or both together, after he has reduced his Bank to zero, any extra hours worked will be paid as overtime which could be voluntary. Thus he has run down his Bank deliberately to start earning extra money. If the on-call rota is not changed then the company might not have the means to cover absences where the swaps of hours into the Bank by the other staff cannot be utilised.

Benefits of Bank Hours

Banked Hours maintains operations with relatively little input from managers and at a fixed cost. The associated methods of using Banked Hours to cover absences mean that a Cover scheme is automatically set up at the same time. The company has a stable environment and the staff have stability of earnings, which mutually benefits both parties.

Absences reduce, and this has the effect of increasing the efficiency of the operation which has the effect of off-setting the costs of purchasing additional Bank Hours.

Training is often a key use of Banked Hours which reduces the number of Covers each person has to do.

Once a year the clocks go back so there is an extra hour. For day employees, it just means an extra hour in bed. For those on night shifts, they have to work an extra hour. The easiest solution is to just pay them an extra hour out of their Bank. However in the Spring when the night shift is an hour shorter, it's not advisable to dock their pay by this hour. It's far too much administration and resentment.

Banked Hours mean employees are brought in to make their work easier when an absence occurs. In this respect, managers and employees are in accord, they want the work to be easy for everyone. Far more people are inconvenienced by an absence than are inconvenienced by a Banked Hours system. This is easy to calculate.

Volunteering for Banked Hours

Whenever a new system is introduced, people are wary of it. Change is always scary, regardless of whether it is a good or a bad change. So, there is likely to be some resistance to it.

Banked Hours when used correctly is good for both the company and the shift workers. However, until people have experienced it, they may not want it.

One way to get around people's natural resistance is to offer to do it by volunteers. You do need a decent percentage of people to volunteer, but not everyone needs to participate.

Let's take an example. You have 100 people on a 24/7 shift operation. We will assume that they are all equally skilled. We will have 20 on per shift, using a holidays included shift pattern. 12-hour shifts, 3% absence rate, contracted to work a 40-hour week with six weeks of holiday.

The company would like there to be three people on cover per day.

Everyone on Banked Hours

If everyone was on Banked Hours, then everyone would be down to work on 146 shifts per year on average. Three people would be needed on cover every day. Therefore, each person would be down to cover on 11 days of the year. This means that on 146 days of the year, they will definitely be coming in to work. On 11 days of the year, they are on cover and may be asked to come in to work on Banked hours. They would each have 88 hours in the bank at the start of the year, on average.

At the end of the year, with a 3% absence rate and the Banked Hours only being used for absence cover, they would expect to have been called in on about five of their cover days. This would mean that they would have received 28 hours of paid time off in exchange for being available on those other 6 days when they were not needed.

50% Volunteer for Banked Hours

If only 50% of the people volunteered to be on the Banked Hours system, then the shift pattern works a little differently. Now 50% of the people need to work their full contracted hours. Hence 50% or 50 people would be down to work 153 shifts in the year.

The 50 volunteers would now be down to work on 139 shifts per year and have a Bank of about 172 hours. However there still needs to be three people on cover every day. The Banked Hours pool is now smaller, so they need to cover 22 days per year. With a 3% absence rate they would be expected to work on about 9 cover days per year. This would mean that they would have received 64 hours of paid time off in exchange for being available on those other 13 days when they were not needed. They get these extra days off when their team is working.

25% Volunteer for Banked Hours

If only 25% of the people volunteered to be on the Banked Hours system, then the shift pattern works a little differently. Now 75% of the people need to work their full contracted hours. Hence 75% or 75 people would be down to work 153 shifts in the year.

The 25 volunteers would now be down to work on 125 shifts per year and have a Bank of about 340 hours. However there still needs to be three people on cover every day. The Banked Hours pool is now smaller, so they need to cover 44 days per year. With a 3% absence rate they would be expected to work on about 17 cover days per year. This would mean that they would have received 136 hours (3 weeks) of paid time off in exchange for being available on those other 27 days when they were not needed.

Comparison

Table 4: Comparison of different percentages of shift workers on Banked Hours

	Scheduled Shifts	Cover Shifts	Worked Shifts	Paid Time Off	Days Off
100% Banked Hours	146	11	151	28h	208
50% without Banked Hours	153	0	153	0	212
50% with Banked Hours	139	22	148	64h	204
75% without Banked Hours	153	0	153	0	212
25% with Banked Hours	125	44	142	136h	196

Table 4 above shows how the different groups would be affected. The more people who are on the Banked Hours system, the less cover shifts each person has to do. However, the reward for being on the Banked Hours system is also smaller. They would be being paid for about 5 hours on the days when they were on call but not needed, just to be ready in case they were needed.

When you consider that most illnesses and absences will be known days in advance, it is a very good bargain, for the shift worker. They are being paid, just to not plan anything on those days. They can still do things around the house, or even do things at the last minute. But that is only on 11 days of the year. They do have 208 days of the year when they know, with certainly, that they will not be asked to come into work.

If only 50% of the people go for Banked Hours, then the 50% without Banked Hours need to work more shifts. They will be scheduled to work the whole of their contracted hours to give the people who did volunteer more days off so that they can be on cover. So, they will work on 153 shifts and have 212 days where they are off.

The 50% who did volunteer for Banked Hours now are down to work less shifts. They are down to work on 139 shifts and 22 cover shifts. With a 3% absence rate, the prediction is that they will work on nine of those 22 cover shifts. So, for the 13 cover shifts when they were on-call but not needed, they were paid for about 5 hours to be prepared to come in if needed. They still have 204 days when they know that the company will not be contacting them.

If only 25% of the people volunteered for Banked Hours, then they would be down to work even less shifts. Only 125 per year. That's about ten shifts per month. They would have to cover about 44 days, when they might be asked to come into work. Of these they would only expect to work on 17 and thus would be paid for about 5 hours on the days when they were not called in, just to be ready to come in if needed. They would still have 196 days off during the year, when they know that they will not be needed to come in and work.

If there is a daily On-Call allowance, then in these three examples it would be that the fewer people on the cover rota, the more money they would receive.

Using Banked Hours to Extend Shifts

Extending shifts is a useful way to cover for holidays, absences, variable workloads and meetings. Coming in on a day off is not always preferable. When you are in work, it is far easier to work a few more hours, than to come in on a day you expected to be off.

Extending shifts to cover for absences and ad-hoc workloads is very popular on 8-hour shifts. It is an easy solution. Doing it with Banked Hours as opposed to overtime is simple. It means that managers are more inclined to cover the absence, so there is less stress because of absence.

If you use 8-hour shifts, then you can easily extend them to 10 or 12-hours. If you use 12-hour shifts, then you can extend them too, however you should be aware that longer shifts have an impact on fatigue. After 12-hours there is a marked decline in alertness. At 16-hours of work, the risk of mistakes or accidents is three times greater than at 8 or 9 hours on shift. So, use caution when extending beyond 12-hours.

If you have three 8-hour shifts to make-up a 24-hour day, these would typically be Early shift 6am-2pm, Late shift 2pm-10pm and Night shift 10pm-6am. So, if someone is absent off one of the shifts, the two shifts on either side, the shift prior and the shift after the absence, can be extended to 12-hours and cover the shortfall.

Hence if the Early shift is absent the 10pm-6am night shift before can be extended to 10am. Then the Late shift can be extended to start early at 10am. So, the Night and the Late shifts are both extended to 12-hours. If one person is absent from a team size of 5, then it would cause 2 people to extend their shifts. If they are all multi-skilled then the on-call person can be anyone. If there are 5 different skills then it might need everyone to be on call, or if a Skills Matrix was in operation, it could be just one person on call.

	06:00 07:00 08:00 09:00 10:00 11:00 12:00 13:00	14:00 15:00 16:00 17:00 18:00 19:00 20:00 21:00 22:00 23:00 00:00 01:00 02:00 03:00 04:00 05:00	06:00 07:00 08:00 09:00 10:00	11:00 12:00 13:00	14:00 15:00 16:00 17:00 18:00 19:00 20:00 21:00
Early Shift	Early Shift		Early Shift (hatched)		
Late Shift		Late Shift		Late Shift (hatched)	Late Shift
Night Shift			Night Shift	Night Shift (hatched)	

Figure 3: Illustration of extending shifts to cover for Early shift absence

The second Early shift in figure 3, is absent. Therefore, the Night shift has been extended (hatching) till 10am and the Late shift has been brought in early at 10am.

If the Late shift is absent the Early shift before can be extended to 6pm. Then the Night shift can be extended to start early at 6pm. So, the Night and the Early shifts are both extended to 12-hours.

	06:00 07:00 08:00 09:00 10:00 11:00 12:00 13:00	14:00 15:00 16:00 17:00 18:00 19:00 20:00 21:00 22:00 23:00 00:00 01:00 02:00 03:00 04:00 05:00	06:00 07:00 08:00 09:00 10:00 11:00 12:00 13:00	14:00 15:00 16:00 17:00 18:00 19:00 20:00 21:00
Early Shift	Early Shift	Early Shift (hatched)	Early Shift	
Late Shift		Late Shift (hatched)		Late Shift
Night Shift		Night Shift (hatched)	Night Shift	

Figure 4: Illustration of extending shifts to cover for Late shift absence

That Late shift in figure 4, is absent. Therefore, the Early shift has been extended (hatching) till 6pm and the Night shift has been brought in early at 6pm.

If the Night shift is absent, then you don't want the shift change over at 2am. Hence the Early shift is extended from 6am-6pm. The Late shift, then starts four hours late and so works from 6pm-6am. So, the Late and the Early shifts are both extended to 12-hours. However, this does rely on the Night shift reporting their absence before the Early shift has left.

	06:00	07:00	08:00	09:00	10:00	11:00	12:00	13:00	14:00	15:00	16:00	17:00	18:00	19:00	20:00	21:00	22:00	23:00	00:00	01:00	02:00	03:00	04:00	05:00	06:00	07:00	08:00	09:00	10:00	11:00	12:00	13:00	14:00	15:00	16:00	17:00	18:00	19:00	20:00	21:00
Early Shift	Early Shift																								Early Shift															
Late Shift											Late Shift																									Late Shift				
Night Shift																	Night Shift																							

Figure 5: Illustration of extending shifts to cover for Night shift absence

The Night shift in figure 5, is absent. Therefore, the Early shift has been extended (hatching) till 6pm. The Late shift has been asked to start late at 6pm and stay till 6am. This will only leave an 8-hour break between Late shifts. So, if the same person is down to work on the late shift on the day when it is extended and the following day, they will need to start late. It is unlikely that there will be a just a single day of absence. Therefore, Late shift would be extended again and work late.

Now when extending shifts, it is normally easier to extend a shift after the shift finish time, than bring someone in early. This is because it will affect their sleeping arrangements, and other activities far more than working late. So how you compensate for the additional hours and how you organise who will work the additional hours, will have a big impact on how easy it is to implement extended shifts.

Example of Using Banked Hours to Extend Shifts

If you use Banked Hours to extend the shifts, you need to identify when and how they will be used. You need to identify who will be working when. Hence you would identify which shift you would extend. You would put them into the schedule.

For example, if you had 100 people covering a 24/7 operation, you could schedule 75 people to come in each day on a holidays excluded option. Of these you might want to have five of them on each of the Early, Late and Night to have the option to extend shifts.

Every day you would rotate the extended shift people, so that the extended shifts were shared out equally between everyone. So, each person on the shift pattern would be scheduled to cover about 55 shifts per year. You could also number the cover shifts, hence each day, you could have the cover shifts numbered one to five on each shift. Where one is the first shift to be extended. So, on each day, everyone knows, who will be asked to work late or start early. This will minimise disruption to the shift worker's lives.

You could use the Extended shifts to cover a variety of absences. A 3% absence rate would mean about 820 absences per year over 100 employees. That would be approximately eight absences each per year. Hence, they would have to extend about 16-17 shifts each.

You could also use Extended Shifts to cover for some holiday. If they all had six weeks of holiday per year, that would be about eight or nine off per day. However, you might need to limit holidays to two off on any shift, so 6 per day. This would not cover for all of their holiday entitlement. So, you might have the remaining time of approximately 800 shifts of holiday. Hence, they would need to extend their shifts on about 15-20 shifts per year for holidays.

Once a shift has been extended, you can pay for the additional hours from the Banked Hours. So, each time they work an extended shift, the number of additional hours they work, is deducted from the Bank.

Some Unions may insist on a payment for being on call. However, extending a shift is not as disruptive to the shift worker's lives as being called in on a day off. But there might be some compensation negotiated. For example, you may take five hours from the Bank for every four hours worked.

This is a very common approach to covering for absences on 8-hour shifts.

Mixed Shift Lengths

Not all shift patterns just use one length of shift. While using just 8 or 12-hour shift is definitely the most common you don't have to be restricted. What some companies do is use a mixture of 8 and 12-hour shifts. They may use 12-hour shifts on weekends as this reduces the number of weekends employees need to work. In effect reducing it by a third, or, doubling their weekends off. On 8-hour shifts they may be working around 31 weekends, after holidays on a 24/7 shift pattern. In comparison if they had 12-hour shifts at weekends, they would only work about 21 weekends, after holidays.

On 12-hour shift patterns you don't have to cover for holidays and absences with 12-hour shifts. Why not provide cover using 8-hour shifts? The shift workers can then book the 8-hour shifts off as holiday if they wish. This means that they can have more days off for the same amount of holiday. If they wish to book a

12-hour shift off as holiday or are absent on a 12-hour shift, then the 8-hour shift that day is extended using Banked Hours to the 12-hour shift.

If the people down to work on the 8-hour shift are not needed for absence or holiday cover, then you are only paying them for 8-hours and not 12-hours. That is a saving of 4-hours which would otherwise be unused.

What's more, 8-hour shifts are far more useful for project work and training.

Let's take an example. You need four people on duty at all times. You don't want to introduce a holiday included shift pattern but you want to make covering for holidays simpler. You have 25 people on your shift pattern each with 6-weeks of holiday per year. Contract hours is 37.5-hours per week.

You want to use 12-hour shifts for the work, but want to use shorter shifts that can then be extended to cover for holidays and absences. You like the 232 shift pattern

So a simple shift pattern would be to have four on each of the 12-hour shifts. 25 people with 6-weeks of holiday is about 6,000 hours of holiday to accommodate. With 8-hour shifts you need to have at least two off on each day.

Therefore, you need three on 8-hour cover shifts each day for holidays. This means that up to three people can be allowed off on holiday on any day. You also need to cover for absence and so you can have a fourth person down to cover for absences.

This means that every day you have four people on a 12-hour Day shifts, four people on 12-hour night shifts and four people on 8-hour shifts which can be changed to either of the 12-hour shifts if needed. If they are not needed than they have a nominal time e.g. 7am-3pm. These shifts are then used for project work or training.

There are 25 people on 37.5-hour week. That is 937.5 hours per week available. They are scheduled to work 896 hours per week. This means that there is a Bank of over 2,000 hours per year available to extend the cover shifts. That's about 86 hours each.

Figure 6 shows an example of how the shift pattern could look with 8 and 12-hour shifts. The D and N shifts are both 12-hours.

The M shifts are 8-hour shifts and can be changed to either of the 12-hour shifts as needed.

On average each person is down to work 175 shifts each per year. Of these about 58 of them will be 12-hour day shifts. About 58 will be 12-hour night shifts and about 58 of them will be the 8-hour cover shifts.

8 & 12							01 January 2025 - 31 December 2025																CDT	
	Start Time	Finish Time	Wednesday	Thursday	Friday		Monday	Tuesday	Wednesday	Thursday	Friday		Monday	Tuesday	Wednesday	Thursday	Friday		Monday	Tuesday	Wednesday	Thursday	Friday
M	07:00	15:00	4	4	4	4	4	4	4	4	4	4	4	4	4	4	4	4	4	4	4	4	4	4
D	07:00	19:00	4	4	4	4	4	4	4	4	4	4	4	4	4	4	4	4	4	4	4	4	4	4
N	19:00	07:00	4	4	4	4	4	4	4	4	4	4	4	4	4	4	4	4	4	4	4	4	4	4
Total			12	12	12	12	12	12	12	12	12	12	12	12	12	12	12	12	12	12	12	12	12	12
P 1	1876	175	N	N	N							N	N				M	M	M		N	N		
P 2	1868	175	N	N	N							M	M								N	N		
P 3	1868	175	N	N	N		M	M				N	N								N	N		
P 4	1864	175	M	M	M							N	N								N	N		
P 5	1876	175	N	N	N							N	N							M	M	M	M	M
P 6	1876	176					N	N		M	M	M		N	N				M	M				
P 7	1880	176					M	M					N	N					M	M			
P 8	1880	176	M	M			N	N					N	N				M	M				
P 9	1888	176					N	N					N	N							M	M	M
P 10	1884	176					N	N					M	M	M	M	M		M	M			
P 11	1856	175	M	M	M		N	N				M	M								N	N	N
P 12	1860	174					N	N					M	M						N	N	N	
P 13	1868	175					N	N		M	M									M	M	M	
P 14	1852	173					N	N				M	M	M	M	M				N	N		
P 15	1876	177					M	M	M	M	M		M	M						N	N		
P 16	1856	174	N	N		M	M								N	N	N						
P 17	1856	174	N	N					M	M					N	N	N		M	M			
P 18	1856	174	N	N		M	M								M	M	M						
P 19	1856	175	N	N					M	M	M	M	M		N	N	N						
P 20	1872	177	M	M	M	M	M		M	M					N	N	N						
P 21	1864	174																	M	M				
P 22	1876	176	M	M			N	N	N				M	M				N	N				
P 23	1852	174							M	M	M								N	N				
P 24	1880	177			M	M	M	M	N	N	N								N	N				
P 25	1880	176	M	M					N	N	N								N	N		M	M	M

Figure 6: Example of 12-hour shifts combined with an 8-hour cover shift

The shift pattern rotates through everyone in turn. The shift pattern is based around five teams of five. So while everyone does work with all of the other teams, they are mainly down to work with their own team.

From the shift workers point of view, they now have lots of choice as to when they can have a holiday. They can have 225 hours of holiday each per year. That is the equivalent of 29 8-hour shifts or 19 12-hour shifts.

If they were P16, in week two they are down to work the M shifts on Monday and Tuesday. If they took these as a holiday, it would cost them about 7% of their holiday and they would have a 10-day break. If they were P19, then they are down to work five M shifts in weeks two and three from Friday to Tuesday. If they took these five shifts off as holiday it would cost them about 17% of their holiday and they could have a 14-day break.

This sort of arrangement encourages people to book the 8-hour shifts as holiday instead of the 12-hour shifts. If they book the 8-hour shifts then they can have more days off than if they booked the 12-hour shifts. If they book the 12-hour shifts then they are inconveniencing their colleagues by making them work longer.

The manager now has very few absence problems. There are four people on each day to cover for holidays and absences. If they need them to extend a shift, they have the Banked Hours available.

They also have a lot of 8-hour shifts available for training and project work.

```
W T F S S M T  W T F S S M T  W T F S S M T  W T F S S M T  W T F S S M T
  N N N           D D              N N          M M M          N N      M M                D D
W T F S S M T  W T F S S M T  W T F S S M T  W T F S S M T  W T F S S M T
  N N N           D D              M M          D D D          N N              M M          D D
W T F S S M T  W T F S S M T  W T F S S M T  W T F S S M T  W T F S S M T
  N N N               M M          N N          D D D          N N      M M                  D D
W T F S S M T  W T F S S M T  W T F S S M T  W T F S S M T  W T F S S M T
  M M M           D D              N N          D D D          N N          M M M M M M
W T F S S M T  W T F S S M T  W T F S S M T  W T F S S M T  W T F S S M T
  N N N           D D              N N          D D D      M M M M M        M M          D D
W T F S S M T  W T F S S M T  W T F S S M T  W T F S S M T  W T F S S M T
  N N N           D D              N N          M M M          N N      M M                D D
W T F S S M T  W T F S S M T  W T F S S M T  W T F S S M T  W T F S S M T
  N N N           D D              M M          D D D          N N              M M          D D
W T F S S M T  W T F S S M T  W T F S S M T  W T F S S M T  W T F S S M T
  N N N               M M          N N          D D D          N N      M M                  D D
W T F S S M T  W T F S S M T  W T F S S M T  W T F S S M T  W T F S S M T
  M M M           D D              N N          D D D          N N          M M M M M M
W T F S S M T  W T F S S M T  W T F S S M T  W T F S S M T  W T F S S M T
  N N N           D D              N N          D D D      M M M M M        M M          D D
W T F S S M T  W T F S S M T  W T F S S M T  W T F S S M T  W T F S S M T
  N N N           D D              N N          M M M          N N          M M          D D
```

Figure 7: Example of annual shift pattern for one person using 12-hour shifts and 8-hour cover shift

Figure 7 shows how the shift pattern would work in practice for the individual. This example show person 1 from figure 6. The days of the week are shown in the odd rows (WTFSSMT Jan 1st 2025 is a Wednesday). The shifts for each day are shown on the even rows (D, N, M). A blank is an unrostered day. At the bottom of the figure the cross hatching shows where the year ends. Figure 7 shows five weeks across starting on Wednesday and finishing on Tuesday.

If the person were to take the two M shifts on Monday and Tuesday in the 4th week, then it would cost 16 hours of holiday and give them a 10-day break.

If they were to book the Wednesday and Thursday Nights shifts in week 9 and the Wednesday and Thursday Morning shifts in week 10. It would cost 40-hours of holiday and they would have a 14-day break.

If they were to book two M shifts on Monday and Tuesday in the 14th week and the Monday and Tuesday Day shifts in week 15, then book the three M shifts in week 16 on Friday, Saturday and Sunday. It would cost 64-hours of holiday and they would have a 19-day break.

Being able to see the whole year at a glance is very helpful for shift workers. They can plan their holidays to maximise their time off. Ideally the full year of shifts would be issued about three months before the start of the year.

Layered Method

You might need to have more than one approach to covering for absences. In the following example there will be three different methods for covering. This example is designed for a key skill. If this skill is not available, then the whole operation will have to stop. Hence a layered approach is needed to ensure that this key skill is always available.

In this example they will be security operatives and the factory needs at least one on duty at all times to comply with their customers' requirements.

In this example there are five people to ensure 24/7 operation plus one manager who can cover as required. The manager is on days Monday-Friday holidays excluded. The rest of the shift workers are on 8-hour shifts with fast turnaround. Normally on 8-hour shifts there is a 16 or 24-hour break between shifts. However sometimes shift workers will request that there is a fast turnaround instead. This is where there is only 8-hours between shifts. Some people like a fast turnaround because they don't mind only having 8-hours between shifts (they might live close and not have much of a commute) and they like having longer breaks. They finish the last shift before a long break 8-hours sooner. They also get compensating rest as soon as they have finished a shift.

There are four shifts in this example, M (Morning), A (Afternoon), N (Night) and D (Day). The Morning shift is a 7-hour shift (7am-2pm), the Afternoon shift is an 8-hour shift (2pm-10pm), the Night shift is a 9-hour shift (10pm-7am) and the Day shift is 8-hours (7am-3pm).

The shifts are different lengths to assist in extending the shifts to cover for absences. 6am is ideal for an 8-hour shift but is not ideal for a 12-hour shift. When considering the start and finish times of shifts, you need to weigh up when the shift will start and finish. So, a 12-hour shift, starting at 6am will finish at 6pm. 6am means that the person will have had 3-hours less sleep, than on a rest day. So, they will be starting the shift tired. On an 8-hour shift they will be able to cope but coping for 12-hours is harder. Also finishing at 6pm is during the rush hour. Therefore, they would be starting the shift tired, working long hours and then driving back in rush hour. This is not ideal. Starting at 7am means that they are more rested. They also finish at 7pm, which is after the rush hour.

The Day shift times means that the manager can observe two shifts each day. They are in for the whole of the Morning shift and see the Afternoon shift for an hour too. Each week the manager would be able to see everyone except the person on holiday.

8 & 12 — 06 January 2025 - 05 January 2026

	Start Time	Finish Time	Monday	Tuesday	Wednesday	Thursday	Friday			Monday	Tuesday	Wednesday	Thursday	Friday			Monday	Tuesday	Wednesday	Thursday	Friday		
D	08:00	16:00	1	1	1	1	1			1	1	1	1	1			1	1	1	1	1		
M	07:00	15:00	1	1	1	1	1	1	1	1	1	1	1	1	1	1	1	1	1	1	1	1	1
A	15:00	22:00	1	1	1	1	1	1	1	1	1	1	1	1	1	1	1	1	1	1	1	1	1
N	22:00	07:00	1	1	1	1	1	1	1	1	1	1	1	1	1	1	1	1	1	1	1	1	1
Total			4	4	4	4	4	3	3	4	4	4	4	4	3	3	4	4	4	4	4	3	3
Manager	2088	261	D	D	D	D	D			D	D	D	D	D			D	D	D	D	D		
Security 1	1785	223	M	M	N	N	A	A	A	M	M	N	N	N	A	A	M	M	M					
Security 2	1770	221					M	M	N	N	N	A	A	M	M	M	N	N	A	A			
Security 3	1750	219	A	A						M	M	M	N	N	A	A							
Security 4	1720	215	N	N	A	A											M	M	N	N	A	A	A
Security 5	1735	217			M	M	N	N	A	A	A	M	M	N	N	N	N						

Figure 8: 232 example shift pattern on 8-hours

Figure 8 shows three weeks of the 232 8-hour shift pattern. The Manager is on the day shift Monday-Friday. The rest of the security team is on the 232 8-hours holidays included shift pattern with fast turnaround. A fast turnaround is when they do not have 11-hours rest between shifts. In this example the night shifts finish at 7am and then the Afternoon shift comes in at 3pm the same day. In the UK there is the requirement that if someone has less than 11 hours rest between shifts, then they receive compensating rest.

Their shift pattern is a five week shift pattern where they work seven consecutive shifts. They work two or three Morning shifts, then have a 31-hour break, before working two or three Night shifts, then have an eight-hour break before working two or three Afternoon shifts. They then have a two-day break, 57 hours, or a 10-day break.

So, they have a 10-day break every five weeks. During the summer, the shift pattern can be changed to give them a 17-day break. The 232-shift pattern is very popular for 8-hour shifts. The fast turnaround version is not as popular because of the 7-hour break.

On 8-hour shifts, they work the majority of days. Therefore, coming in to cover for an absence on one of their precious days off has limited appeal. Most organisations with this type of arrangement will convert the 8-hour shifts to 12-hours.

They are on a 40-hour week. They have 30-days of holiday. So, on average they would have 93-hours in their Bank to cover for absences. This is about 5% of their contracted hours.

Table 5 shows how to cover for an absence. It can apply at any time, for as long as the illness lasts, to any of the five staff on shift. For ease of understanding, I have selected the first week in the shift pattern shown in figure 8 and table 5 starts with the first shift of that week worked by the first person. There are usually several ways to cover for each absence and it would be the responsibility of the Line Manager to select the preferred method of cover depending on the circumstances. These circumstances can include; the number of consecutive absent shifts; the shifts on days immediately before and after the absence.

The normal shifts are M, A, N and the 12hr shifts are denoted as D12 and N12 with their times being 7am-7pm and 7pm-7am.

Most absences are longer than a single shift, a cold for instance can mean that staff are off for a week. In these cases, it will always be possible to implement the preferred action above for the 1st day of absence. However, in some cases this stops the preferred action being possible on the 2nd day of absence. Also possible is that the change on a preceding day sets up a different preferred option for the second day. By and large, the more that is known about the possible absence duration the easier the planning of the covering shifts.

Therefore, we always recommend that **all absences must be reported as soon as they are known**. Even if this is on a day off. They should also report how long they think they will be off work for and update work as and when these estimates are changed. This means that their colleagues have less disruption to their lives.

The case against having several methods is that staff will know that there are several methods using different staff in different ways. So, if they are called to cover an absence, they can ask that the other cover methods are tried instead. However, if there is only one method, then because of the nature of absences being unplanned, allied with the fact that at least two shifts have to change to cover the absence, and that there are three shifts each day, then all staff have to be able to respond every day. This would be far too restrictive and would not be acceptable to the staff. Thus, a balance needs to be struck between the need for cover and the staff's need for stability.

For some shifts there isn't an alternative, such as Saturday Night. In the example above, it would be unlikely that Security 4, Security 5 or Manager would like to work it without a prior agreement that they can be called in.

Table 5: Response to Absence with Extended Shifts

Absent shift	First Preferred Action	Second Preferred Action	Third Preferred Action
Monday M	Security 4 N changed to D12, Security 3 changed to N12	Manager changed to M	Security 2 Day Off changed to A, Security 4 changed to M, Security 3 changed to N
Monday A	Security 1 changed to D12, Security 4 changed to N12	Security 2 Day Off changed to A	
Monday N	Security 1 changed to D12, Security 3 changed to N12		
Tuesday M	Security 4 Monday N changed to 11pm-11am, Security 3 A changed to 11am-11pm	Manager changed to M	Security 2 Day Off changed to M
Tuesday A	Security 1 changed to D12, Security 4 changed to N12		
Tuesday N	Security 1 changed to D12, Security 4 changed to N12		
Wednesday M	Security 1 changed to D12, Security 4 changed to N12	Manager changed to M	Security 3 Day Off changed to A, Security 1 changed to M, Security 4 changed to N
Wednesday A	Security 2 changed to D12, Security 1 changed to N12	Security 3 Day Off changed to A	
Wednesday N	Security 2 changed to D12, Security 4, changed to N12		
Thursday M	Security 1 Wednesday N changed to 11pm-11am, Security 4 A changed to 11am-11pm	Manager changed to M	Security 3 Day Off changed to M
Thursday A	Security 2 changed to D12, Security 1 changed to N12		
Thursday N	Security 2 changed to D12, Security 4 changed to N12		
Friday M	Security 2 changed to D12, Security 1 changed to N12	Manager changed to M	Security 4 Day Off changed to A, Security 2 changed to M, Security 1 changed to N
Friday A	Security 3 changed to D12, Security 2 changed to N12	Security 4 Day Off changed to A	
Friday N	Security 3 changed to D12, Security 1 changed to N12		
Saturday M	Security 2 Friday N changed to 11pm-11am, Security 1 A changed to 11am-11pm	Manager or Security 4 Day Off changed to M	
Saturday A	Security 3 changed to D12, Security 2 changed to N12	Manager or Security 4 Day Off changed to A	
Saturday N	Security 3 changed to D12, Security 1 changed to N12, Security 3 Sunday M changed to D12, Security 1 Sunday A changed to 7pm-11pm		
Sunday M	Security 2 Saturday N changed to 11pm-11am, Security 1 changed to 11am-11pm	Manager or Security 5 Day Off changed to M	
Sunday A	Security 3 changed to D12, Security 2 changed to N12	Manager Day Off changed to A	
Sunday N	Security 3 changed to D12, Security 1 changed to N12		

Sent Home Policy

Sometimes companies don't always know what the workload for the day will be until the day occurs. Therefore, they might staff for the average and try to bring people in if needed or send people home if not. Examples we have worked on, include ship's pilots and dock gangs where they are dependent on the tides and weather. Aircraft maintenance dependent on weather and general delays in air traffic. Train maintenance, cleaning, repairs, refueling. Hotels.

This form of staffing is not very popular with shift workers. They never know when they will be working. An on-call system helps with bringing people in, but how do you send people home if they are not needed?

Firstly, the system needs to be fair. You need to create a flexible shift or U-shift. These shifts need to be shared out equally between everyone, so that no one is unfairly penalized. These shifts need to be mixed in with shifts where they know in advance that they will be working.

There needs to be rules concerning who will be sent home, and when.

Let's take an example, where you know you will need an average of five people on 24/7 over the year. However, you won't know until closer to the day, how many you will need on each day. You may need five, or you may need three if there is little work, or seven if there is a lot of work. This is typical order profile in industries with *just in time* processes such as food producers for supermarkets. This is where an order comes in at midnight for delivery 32 hours later. The food producer then sets up the operation that produces at least the right order quantity using the minimum resources.

How many people should you employ? How can you create a schedule which will accommodate this sort of fluctuation? Well in this case the average doesn't help us much. We need the distribution across all of the variations. So, we need data, the more data the better with complicated workloads.

Let's say that last year on 10 days of the year, three people were required, on 60 days of the year, four people were required, on 130, five people were needed, on 100 days they needed six and on 65 days they needed seven.

Five people may be the average, but they do need more than that. Since they only need three people on ten days, let's say that they will not go below four people at all times. The data shows that they are probably better off going for six on at all times and then having two people on call if they need seven and sending people home if they need five or four people on.

The hours they save when there are four or five people on can then pay for the times when they need seven people on. So, every day, if we use 12-hour shifts, there are four people on flexible shifts (two on day, two on night). There are four people on days, and four people on nights. There is also one person on day call cover and one person on night call in.

If they were paid for 12-hours per shift, then on a 38-hour week with six weeks of holidays included, they would need 30 people on the shift pattern.

They would then each be scheduled for 170 shifts per year. Of these about 24 would be cover shifts where they could be brought in to work a day or a night shift and bring the total number of workers to seven. About 48 shifts would be flexible, where they could be stood down as needed and their hours added to the bank to cover the call-in shifts when seven people were needed. The remainder, about 97 shifts would be either day or night shifts when they knew they would be working.

Therefore, the company would be paying for 30 people to do the work of about 28 people. However, they don't know when these people would be needed. So they are employing two extra people to give them this flexibility.

Since this would create a Bank of about 160 hours each at the end of the year, the company might want to use those hours to provide absence cover as well as covering for the ad-hoc workload variation.

If they had a 3% absence rate, this is about 55hrs each per year. They may also want to increase the number of call-in shifts to three per day to cover for absences when seven people are needed.

Hence the shift workers would receive about 100 hours off for being available to the company on 183 days per year on average. Of which they would be covering about 36 days when they might be needed as the seventh person on shift.

So, the company can cover their variable workload and cover for absences all at basic rate. They also have spare capacity in the system so that if there is an increase in the workload, they can cope with the current operation. They could cover the workload at basic rate even if the workload increased by up to 6%. Thus, they have gained a very flexible arrangement.

Crediting for being sent home

If a person is not needed, it is far better for most organisations to send them home on full pay, than try to incorporate them into the operation. There are exceptions to this, if there is secondary work e.g. project work, or for security firms where they just send them out on patrol more often. But if you have a person stood around doing nothing, it is very distracting to managers and the other people on shift. The person who is doing nothing gets bored. The manager wants to include them. If they are included, then the whole operation needs to be reorganised to accommodate an extra body and this takes time. If the shift gets used to working with one extra person then they can start to struggle when the correct number of people is used.

Hence if you can send someone home why not? The shift worker would like to receive full pay for the shift even if they didn't work it. But you could negotiate. Why not give them an hour or two's credit for coming into work and then bank the rest of the hours.

Provided it was limited to a small number of shifts per year, you can gain a large amount of flexibility and then use those hours when needed, instead of trying to reorganise the whole operation because you have an extra person for a few hours.

On 8-hour shifts, days off are very precious because people have so few of them. Weekends are especially precious. So, having more paid time off is an excellent reward for working a few extra hours on another shift.

It is like a *Golden Days* system. *Golden Days* are set up when companies move to a holidays included shift operation. Very often people are nervous about starting a completely new way of working. Therefore, a *Golden Days* system is introduced. Most of the holidays are included in the rota. However about three to five days per person are not. These days are called *Golden Days*. These *Golden Days* can be taken at any time by the shift workers subject to the negotiated rules.

This means that while the vast majority of the holidays are included in the shift pattern, should someone need a day off at another time e.g. birthday, anniversary, football match, then they can have a Golden day off.

So over rostering and then allowing people to have days off, is very similar to a holidays excluded operation, only the problem is a lot smaller and thus easier to manage.

Shift Workers are familiar with this type of operation and are therefore happy to move onto the scheme. As they work the extra hours, they gain a Golden Day equivalent to a shift, be it 8 or 12 hours. Thus several accounting systems can operate at the same time with several Banks. As they work additional hours, these can come from the Bank or can set up future time off. If they are sent home, the hours can go into the Bank to be used later on.

Requesting Days Off

Sometimes a company changes the emphasis as to who is sent home. They over roster their staff and then allow *them* to request days off when they are not needed. These days off are taken in agreement to pre-arranged rules.

Shift Workers like this sort of arrangement. This is no ambiguity over when they are working. They know when they are working, much like a normal shift roster. They can then take days off in a similar method to the usual way of booking holidays.

They can only have these days off when the work is low or there is sufficient cover e.g. a manager is on duty to cover. They may not always take a full shift. They may take only half a shift off at a time. They may request to take half a shift off before they leave for an extended holiday. They may request half a shift off when they are expecting a delivery or need to visit the bank etc.

This type of flexible arrangement can work well for both the company and the employees. Employees feel that they have greater flexibility and the company has the people when they need them.

Productivity

Flexible working has long been associated with increasing productivity. If you pay people for only the hours that you need, then they will be more productive than having them sat around waiting for work. So the more flexible you make the workforce, there is the potential to increase productivity.

Variable Length Shifts

Extending shifts with overtime and banked hours has already been discussed. As has sending people home when you don't need them.

You could also use different length shifts to match the workload. For example if you do not have a flat workload, but a workload that varies over the day, then you can get a closer match by using different length shifts. The best way to demonstrate this is with an example.

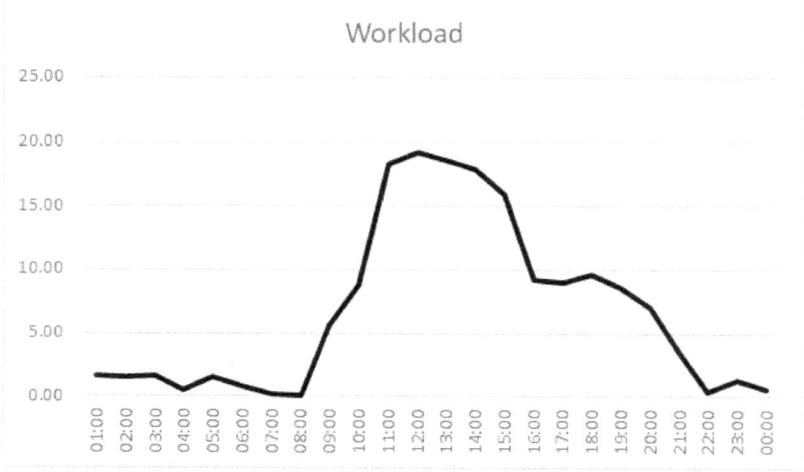

Figure 9: Variable workload over the day

If you have a workload like figure 9, with staffing requirement on the left and time of day at the bottom, then you have very low workload over the night. From 8am the work starts to ramp up, peaking at noon. This is a typical workload for anyone who has to interact with the public. So how do you match the shifts?

If you only used 8-hour shifts then you would need shifts to start at 4 different times:

- 6am: 10 people start (6am-2pm)
- 10am: 10 people start (10am-6pm)
- 2pm: 10 people start (2pm-10pm)
- 10pm: 2 people start (10pm-6am)

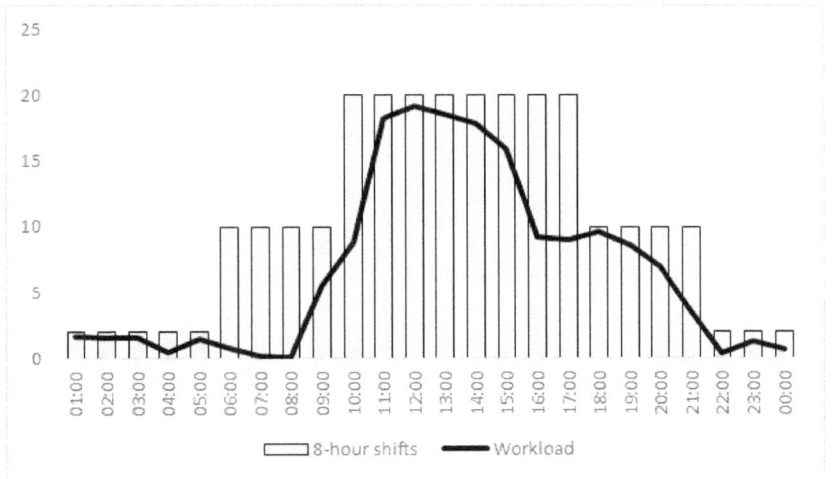

Figure 10: Variable workload over the day covered with 8-hour shifts

Figure 10 shows the staffing levels against the workload over the day. The pale grey columns are the staffing levels and the black line is the workload in figure 9.

So the workload is covered, however there are lots of times during the day when you would be overstaffed. Being over staffed is not good. First of all it costs more. Secondly if people have nothing to do, then they will get bored. Studies have shown that being underworked is just as tiring as being overworked.

Would a different length of shift help?

N.B. This example is based on a requirement that staff are available with a short delay such as emergency services. Where a long delay is possible you might staff to an average workload.

Figure 11 shows the workload covered with different length shifts. There is a 10-hour shift over night with 2 people. Then there is an 8am 8-hour shift with 10 people and finally a 12-hour shift starting at 10am.

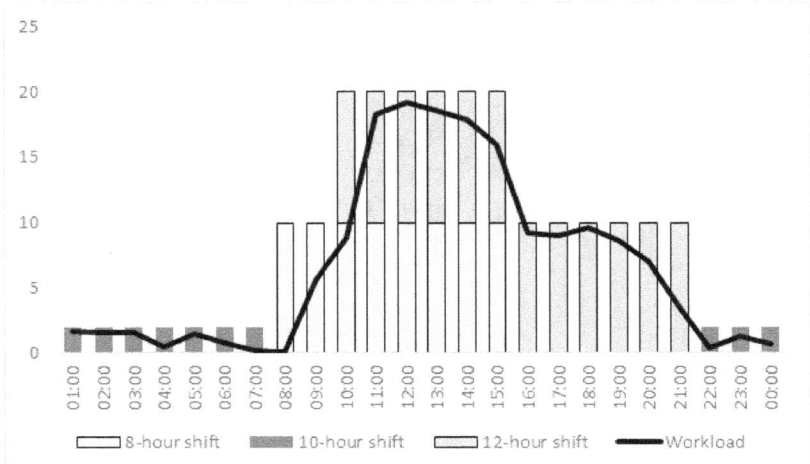

Figure 11: Variable workload over the day covered with different length shifts

By changing the lengths of the shifts we end up with a closer match to the workload. This means that it would cost less. With 8-hour shifts it would take 256 hours per day to cover the workload. With a mixture of shifts it only takes 220 hours per day to cover the workload. This results in a saving of 36 hours per day or 14%. If these people were paid £10 per hour then over a year you would save £131,400.

Variations over the Year

Most staffing schedules are designed for flat workloads which will only change gradually. Yet workloads are rarely flat. Even in production there will be times of years where different products are made, e.g. Summer products and Christmas products. So why not have a staffing schedule that responds as you need it, yet creates stability for the workforce so that they will know what they are working a long time in advance?

The first step is to calculate your workload for every day over the whole year. Look out for commonalities, so if Sunday is always the same throughout the year, then treat them the same. Look out for one-off events, like the annual clean/maintenance or product promotions. Some changes will have to be at short notice like variations in the weather or if your customer runs a promotion. These can be estimated for over the year.

Then you match the staffing levels to the workload. So if the workload is lower over the winter, then they work less hours over the winter and more in the summer months.

As an example let's have a University security team. The terms are:

- Autumn Term: Monday 26th September – Friday 16th December (12 weeks)
- Spring Term: Monday 16th January – Friday 31st March (11 weeks)
- Summer Term: Tuesday 2nd May – Friday 23rd June (8 weeks)

Let's have them working 12-hour shifts. 10 people are required at night throughout the year. Then 10 people are required during the day for holiday periods. During term time they have 20 people Monday to Friday and 15 people at weekends. In the first two weeks of the Autumn term they need 30 people on during the day. This is to look after the new students. There will also be one-off days requiring additional personnel on duty, such as Graduation Day or a visit by a dignitary

If they are on 40 hours per week on average what would the shift pattern look like for the individual?

First we need to look at the hours over the year. The overall workload would be 111,480 hours. Therefore we need ~60 security guards for the year.

Figure 12 shows an example of how the shift pattern could look for the security team. In this example most of the time they are working the 232 shift pattern. I have set up the operation so they all have lots of weeks off in addition to their holidays. In this example they have 5 weeks off in the year. So the pattern is easy to work and matches the workload.

In this example D is the Day shift and N is the Night shift. In the real situation we would have different starting times for the Day and Night shifts to provide overlaps during shift change overs especially in the Control Room.

A key feature of all Security Operations is the ability to be able to respond to two simultaneous security events. It is a well known practice to create a diversion to enable the real security event to take place. This requirement usually means that breaks on shift are staggered and holidays are restricted. This is especially the case on Nights as in this example we have a reduced number of Security Officers on duty for budgeting purposes. Of the initial 10 Officers each night, one is likely to be on holiday, often one will be absent and one will be on a break. This leaves seven Officers, so we would have two in the Control Room, and five on Patrol over the campus before the event. If an incident occurred, such as a fire alarm or a theft or a car accident, two or three Officers would attend depending on the incident. The remaining two or three Officers would be recalled to the Control Room in case the event was a diversion. This would be the Standard Operating Procedure.

As a backup, the local Police Force would be alerted to take over if the event was criminal in nature or the Fire Brigade would be called in if there was a fire alarm event or a car accident. These would require additional Security Officers to look after them. So you can see a small event can easily lead to an escalation using all Officers.

By varying the staffing levels over the year we can ensure that there are enough people for the predicted workloads and reduce fatigue from being over or under worked.

Figure 12: Example shift pattern

Job and Knock

There is a saying, "Job and Knock" which means that you do the job and then knock off work. It's an old saying for workers who are paid to do a job, not paid for the amount of time they are at work. Hence when they have finished the work, they are free to go home.

You can use this method of working when you don't know the length of a job. Let's say we are discussing repair jobs, the average time it takes to go out and do a "job" is five hours. Hence in an 8-hour shift you can do one job on average, on a 10-hour shift you could do two jobs. On a 12-hour shift you could still do two jobs on average.

So how long should a shift be? Well the average length of a job is a very good indication, but it is also dependent on when these jobs come in. So, if you are given a list of jobs in the morning, then a 10-hour shift would mean that you could do two jobs in one shift. If on the other hand you are waiting for the jobs to come in, then a 12-hour shift, would mean that you can wait an hour or two before the first job comes in and still get two jobs done in a shift.

The other thing to consider is what happens if a job takes longer than the average. So, the person gets to a job, it's five hours before the end of their shift, and the job takes about seven hours. Do they stay late and finish the job? Or do they go home at the end of their shift and then have to return the next day?

If they come in the next day, there is the travel time to consider if it is off site, the setting up and closing down of the work. If they leave a job midway through it could be dangerous. Wires could be exposed, there is the risk that someone else damages the equipment during the night. Or maybe the repair person is not due to come back onto shift for several days. In which case tomorrow, it will be someone else doing the job. They may take longer as they are unfamiliar with the work. There is also the inconvenience to the customer. "Sorry I can't finish it today, but I'm off home now. Someone will be along to finish the job hopefully tomorrow!" Doesn't lead to customer satisfaction.

So, it is normally better to pay overtime and have the engineer stay late. However, you are then incentivizing people to take longer to do the jobs. What should take five hours to complete, may now take 5.5 hours. Therefore, on average they have an hour of overtime every shift.

This can very quickly spiral out of control and lead to an overtime culture.

Banked Hours with Job and Knock

What about incentivizing people to finish the work quicker. That is what "Job and Knock" is all about.

Let's say that on average a job takes five hours. The jobs come in before the engineers, so they don't have to wait around. They come in and are sent straight off on a job, or just call in and are sent off on a job. Therefore, the shift length is set at 10-hours. They work four shifts in a week on average. That is a 40-hour week. However, let's say you pay them for a 42-hour week. Therefore, each year they will have a Bank of hours. This Bank would contain 104 hours on average, (2.5 weeks). Then if a job took longer than the average 5-hours, it's not a problem. They just stay late and finish the job. The extra hours are paid for from their Bank. There is now no incentive for making the job take longer. There is now an incentive for doing the work quicker. If they get all of their allotted jobs done within the shift, they can go home early with no penalties. If they take longer, they have to stay until the job is finished. They get no additional pay, until they have worked all of the extra hours in their Bank.

Now you do have to have lots of safeguards in place. You don't want your engineers to do a careless job just to finish quicker. You don't want the same people sent out on the quicker jobs all of the time because they are the coordinator's favourites.

However, if planned correctly, you end up with a more efficient system. Your workers do not have any incentive for dragging out the work. You no longer pay any overtime. Your engineers are happier, they are being paid to be at home for another 2.5 weeks per year. Your customers are happier, you not only get the work done in one day, but the engineers always stay late to finish the job. You can even have the motto that *you never leave a job unfinished*.

So, you have a cheaper, more efficient operation. Your employees and customers are happy. You are reliable and good. So now your only problem is trying to keep up with demand.

Clearing the backlog

From time to time every company will experience a backlog. Even 999 call centers and the ambulance service which tries to deal with emergencies immediately by having more people than the workload, will experience a backlog. This is because either your supply or your demand will vary over time. You can't always anticipate this. Therefore demand will outstrip supply and a backlog will start to build up.

Call centres are an easy example to demonstrate what happens. If we have a call centre with a call rate of 300 calls per hour and each call takes 120 seconds (2minutes) to deal with the call from start to wrap up. Simple maths show that you would need 10 call operators to handle the workload.

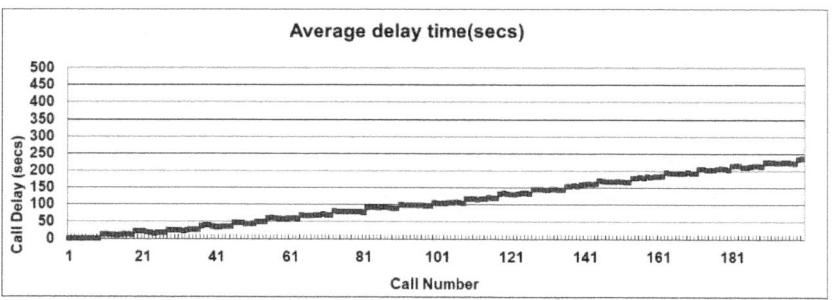

Figure 13: Call delay if operators are reduced by one

Now if one of these operators goes on a break for 30 minutes, the call delay would increase. Figure 13 shows how the delay builds up over the 30 minute break. At the end of the 30 minutes there would be about 20 calls waiting to be answered. That's over 13% of the calls that arrived in that half hour. That figure may surprise you as the missing operator would mean that only 15 calls weren't handled immediately. What happens in practice is that when the operator goes for a break, there are still 150 calls that come in and the first 9 calls have no delay. However the 10th call is now answered late as there isn't a free operator. The same happens for the 11th call, it is also delayed. And so on for all the calls, which is what you see in the graph, every single call has a delayed response and the delay gets longer and longer through the 30 minutes. The delay in answering the calls become longer than the call duration and at the end of the 30 minutes the delay is so long that there are 20 calls waiting for an operator at the end of the 30 minute break. Also of note is that every call is experiencing a three minute delay in being answered at the end of the 30 minutes. The above graph is calculated with a random input time and a random call duration, just as it happens in the real world.

Of course in the practical world, unless you had 30 lines for the callers, you wouldn't even know how many just got the busy signal. That's 10 being answered and 20 waiting.

When faced with this sort of problem, the easiest way to solve it is to run simulations using the real call data. Then we can ascertain the best number of operators to employ. Alternatively to ascertain the number of missed calls given the number of operators.

Having simulated the outcome of the various ways in which a reduction in staffing has on the business, it is then much easier to justify bringing in additional resources. Holidays, absences, training days, meetings, leave, promotions and all the other ways that affect staffing levels can be covered by Banked Hours.

Backlogs are inevitable, your workload is variable and at some point it will overwhelm the available resources for a period of time. If you staff for the average workload you will always have a backlog of work, it's inevitable. If you staff for slightly higher than the average workload you will still have backlogs on a regular basis. Banked Hours gives you the means to have extra resources at your disposal to cope with the backlogs.

Busy days and identifying them early.

In our analysis of variable workloads for organisations, we have noted a phenomena that can be used to identify days that will be much busier than average. In fig.10 we can see how the work ramps up from about 10am and we see this many times in urgent work that comes in from the public and when there are SLAs of several hours. For example utility services. What we see on days that we would later class as being 'busy' is that the ramping up starts a few hours earlier than usual. So if you see the same level of activity between 8am-9am as you would expect to see between 11am-12pm, then the day becomes a 'busy' day. For instance you might set up the resources to handle 200 jobs per day. These might be utilities, ATM failures, printing failures, and many other types of jobs connected with the public. Being on the lookout for busy days enables you to bring in extra resources using Banked Hours before you are overwhelmed.

Another source of busy days is weather connected such as a storm. Storms bring down trees onto power lines and rain causes local flooding. The storms hitting Europe start five days earlier in the Caribbean and North America. We can watch these approaching, we can give them a name, and then see them hit Europe. With five days notice, we can set in place an appropriate response to a fairly common problem, that is having enough people in place before the storm hits. Storms have a 'front' and they have a width and we can use that information. It is also about having the right equipment, chain saws and pumps, in place to handle the work. We can put all the planned work on hold in order to move the resources to where the storm will hit the hardest. We can call in everyone on Banked Hours and move them to the right place at the right time. Or we can wait until after the storm hits and react accordingly. I remember one UK analysis we did after the event some 20 years ago where we mapped the calls coming in as a speeded up real time movie. By plotting the postcodes of the calls we could see the effects of the wind and the rain on power lines and cables. We saw the speed and width of the destruction as it moved over Wales and then England at a steady pace. Knowing in advance where and when people will be needed, even by a few hours, is extremely useful when deploying limited resources. In this instance overtime was used to bring in the extra resources, however overtime does not guarantee resources as there is an element of choice. In addition to having the resources, there also needs to be a plan about the timing of the use of the resources. These resources are most efficiently utilised in day light hours when all the skills and control personnel are present. This would restore power in the shortest time. However politically it is impossible to have anything other than a 24-hour presence which means dispersing the resources over time. This is difficult to manage using voluntary overtime but isn't a problem using Banked Hours as the staff go where they are directed over the 24-hours.

Annual Excess Hours

Excess Hours are hours worked over and above their contracted hours. This can normally only be determined at the end of each year as to how many hours a person has worked in comparison to their contract. Sometimes a shift pattern will roll over the end of the year. So if they work more hours in one year then they will work less hours in another year. These additional hours are not considered excess hours if they rotate around the average.

Regular overtime

One way to cope with holidays and absences is to use overtime. The advantages of this are that you don't need to employ additional workers or train up individuals if the skill set is rare. The disadvantages are that it is expensive with overtime rates usually being between 1.5 to 2 times basic rate, and there is the problem of overworking the individuals. When an individual is already working between 37 to 48 hours per week, creating a shift pattern which gives the individual a good work-life balance, meets the Working Time Directive, and allows for additional overtime, can be problematic.

			Mon 05-Sep	Tue 06-Sep	Wed 07-Sep	Thu 08-Sep	Fri 09-Sep	Sat 10-Sep	Sun 11-Sep	Mon 12-Sep	Tue 13-Sep	Wed 14-Sep	Thu 15-Sep	Fri 16-Sep	Sat 17-Sep	Sun 18-Sep	Mon 19-Sep	Tue 20-Sep	Wed 21-Sep	Thu 22-Sep	Fri 23-Sep	Sat 24-Sep	Sun 25-Sep
D 07:00 21:00			2	2	2	2	2	2	2	2	2	2	2	2	2	2	2	2	2	2	2	2	2
C 07:00 07:00			1	1	1	1	1	1	1	1	1	1	1	1	1	1	1	1	1	1	1	1	1
N 21:00 07:00			2	2	2	2	2	2	2	2	2	2	2	2	2	2	2	2	2	2	2	2	2
Total			5	5	5	5	5	5	5	5	5	5	5	5	5	5	5	5	5	5	5	5	5
Names	Hours Worked	Shifts Worked																					
Team 1	2196	229	D	D		C							D	D		C	C				D	D	D
Team 2	2184	228			D	D		C	C					D	D	D	C				D	D	D
Team 3	2196	228					D	D	D	C					D	D	C						
Team 4	2184	227	C							D	D					N		D	D	C			
Team 5	2196	228	D	D	C								D	D	C						D	D	D
Team 6	2184	227		D	D	C								D	D	D		C					
Team 7	2196	229					D	D	D	C						D	D	C					
Team 8	2184	229	C					D	D	C						D	D	C		C		

Figure 14: 232 Shift Pattern with overtime shifts

Here are three different 12-hour shift patterns to cope with this. You could also use 8-hour shifts and extend the shifts on each side of the missing shift by 4 hours to cover. Using 12-hour shifts it is often impractical to extend the shifts therefore whole cover shifts must be added.

The 12-hour shift patterns show 8 Teams instead of the usual 4 Teams. This is because it can illustrate how the Cover shifts can be distributed over several people in each team.

D	07:00	21:00		2	2	2	2	2	2	2	2	2	2	2	2	2	2	2	2	2	2	2	2
C	07:00	07:00		1	1	1	1	1	1	1	1	1	1	1	1	1	1	1	1	1	1	1	1
N	21:00	07:00		2	2	2	2	2	2	2	2	2	2	2	2	2	2	2	2	2	2	2	2
Total				5	5	5	5	5	5	5	5	5	5	5	5	5	5	5	5	5	5	5	5
				Mon	Tue	Wed	Thu	Fri	Sat	Sun	Mon	Tue	Wed	Thu	Fri	Sat	Sun	Mon	Tue	Wed	Thu	Fri	Sat	Sun
Names	Hours Worked	Shifts Worked		05-Sep	06-Sep	07-Sep	08-Sep	09-Sep	10-Sep	11-Sep	12-Sep	13-Sep	14-Sep	15-Sep	16-Sep	17-Sep	18-Sep	19-Sep	20-Sep	21-Sep	22-Sep	23-Sep	24-Sep	25-Sep
Team 1	2196	229	D	D	D	C										D	D	D			C	C		
Team 2	2184	228	C								D	D	D				C	C						
Team 3	2196	228							D	D	D		C	C								D	D	D
Team 4	2184	227				D	D	D		C	C							D	D	D	C		
Team 5	2196	229	D	D	D		C	C							D	D	D		C				
Team 6	2184	229	C	C							D	D	D		C								
Team 7	2196	228							D	D	D	C									D	D	D
Team 8	2184	227				D	D	D	C									D	D	D		C	C

Figure 15: 3on-3off Shift Pattern with overtime shifts

D	07:00	21:00		2	2	2	2	2	2	2	2	2	2	2	2	2	2	2	2	2	2	2	2	2
C	07:00	07:00		1	1	1	1	1	1	1	1	1	1	1	1	1	1	1	1	1	1	1	1	1
N	21:00	07:00		2	2	2	2	2	2	2	2	2	2	2	2	2	2	2	2	2	2	2	2	2
Total				5	5	5	5	5	5	5	5	5	5	5	5	5	5	5	5	5	5	5	5	5
				Thu	Fri	Sat	Sun	Mon	Tue	Wed	Thu	Fri	Sat	Sun	Mon	Tue	Wed	Thu	Fri	Sat	Sun	Mon	Tue	Wed	Thu	Fri
Names	Hours Worked	Shifts Worked		01-Sep	02-Sep	03-Sep	04-Sep	05-Sep	06-Sep	07-Sep	08-Sep	09-Sep	10-Sep	11-Sep	12-Sep	13-Sep	14-Sep	15-Sep	16-Sep	17-Sep	18-Sep	19-Sep	20-Sep	21-Sep	22-Sep	23-Sep
Team 1	2208	230	D	D	C					D	D	C				D	D	C				
Team 2	2196	229		D	D	C					D	D	C				D	D	C				
Team 3	2184	228			D	D	C					D	D	C				D	D	C			
Team 4	2184	227				D	D	C					D	D	C				D	D	C		
Team 5	2184	227					D	D	C					D	D	C				D	D	C	
Team 6	2184	227						D	D	C					D	D	C				D	D	
Team 7	2184	228	C					D	D	C					D	D	C					D
Team 8	2196	229	D	C				D	D	C					D	D	C				

Figure 16: DDCNN Shift Pattern with overtime shifts

On the 232 shift pattern the cover shifts are worked between the days and nights, so that both day and night shifts can be covered. They could work up to seven consecutive shifts, however here the shift pattern is designed so that they only work up to four consecutive shifts with single days off. Figure 14 shows the 232 with cover shifts which can be converted to overtime shifts. The shifts are rotated so that there are days off.

On the 3on-3off shift pattern again the cover shifts can be worked between the day and night shifts. However it is possible they could be working up to nine consecutive shifts. Figure 15 shows the 3on-3off shift pattern with cover shifts which can be converted to overtime shifts. The shifts are rotated to limit the number of consecutive shifts.

Figure 16 is an example of how a 4on-4off shift pattern can be set up to limit the number of consecutive shift. The individual works two days, one cover, two nights, three off. This is an eight day rotation. However they will only be working up to five consecutive shifts.

On all of these options everyone does not have to work all of the overtime shifts every week. Individuals can select a proportion of overtime shifts they would be willing to work each year; these are then incorporated into the shift pattern at the start of the year. This way the company always has overtime shifts available and the shift workers always have guaranteed dates when they will not be required to work.

This means that you can increase your workforce by up to 25%. So if you have a backlog, a peak in the workload or lots of holidays to cover, you can flex your workforce to meet demand without employing extra people. This is especially important if you only need it for a short period of time or the skills required are scarce.

Excess Hours with Banked Hours

Banked Hours are like money in the bank. You can have a positive or negative balance. If the Banked Hours are positive, then the employee owes hours to the company. If the Banked Hours are negative, then the company owes hours to the employee.

When the company owes the employee, there are several things that can be done. This depends partly on why there is a negative balance, and when the negative balance occurs. The most common reasons for a negative balance are:

1. Over scheduled hours at the start of the year
2. High absence or loss of staff
3. Unbalanced workload or shift pattern

The reason for the negative hours affects how the company will compensate their employees. The easiest solution is to pay for the excess hours at overtime rate. So, if at the end of the year the employee is owed 15 hours, then they can be paid at an average overtime rate.

For small random excess hours, paying overtime, is simple. However, when there is a consistent level of negative Banked Hours, or very high levels of owed Banked Hours, overtime is not always the best policy.

Time off in lieu

Banked Hours is an easy way to manage time off in lieu. Some employers give their employees time off instead of paying for overtime. This is known as 'time off in lieu'. If a person works excess hours in one period, then they can be given this time off at another time. Hence on average they are working their contracted hours, but within each period, they are either working more or less than their contracted hours.

The Banked Hours system highlights when people are scheduled to work more than their contracted hours. So, the manager can make a decision. The manager can either decide to pay for the excess hours or decide to allow the employee more time off in exchange. This can be either a formal or an informal arrangement.

Some companies deliberately over schedule employees because the workload is unknown at the start of the year. Then when the workload is reduced, employees can request time off in lieu.

The time off in lieu can be in whole shifts, or in part shifts. For example, if a company requires two operators on at all times, but the contracted hours of their current employees are insufficient so they only allow for this 95% of the time (which often happens when shift patterns are changed), they may decide to roster everyone to ensure that there are two people on duty at all times, thus creating negative Banked Hours. Then the operators can request days off. This could be when a manager is there to cover for their absence. For example, Monday to Friday, on Day shifts only. Or they might be allowed to reduce their shift lengths by two hours or only work half a shift provided there is always one person on duty and the workload that week is predicted to be low.

Hence the employees would start off the year with a negative Bank of hours, but have a zero Bank at the end of the year.

One company required occasional Saturday working, but it was unpredictable. So they scheduled in a skeleton crew for every Saturday of the year which initially caused their annual hours to exceed their contracted hours. Then as each Saturday approached, they could stand-down some or all of the employees according to how much work there was. This removed several problems: they didn't need to pay overtime for

Saturdays and they didn't have to beg people to work at short notice.

In another example, a company had batched production. Each week they had a different number of products to make. In most weeks the work could be done Monday-Friday. However, some batches would take longer or if there was a break down, and the work ran into the weekend. As weekend working was unpredictable, they changed the shift pattern. The operation was changed to run over seven days not five. Hence if they were not needed at the weekends, the shifts could be moved to the following week, Monday to Friday. This would mean that they could reduce overtime at weekends, and incentivise the shift workers to finish the work within the week. The shift workers were paid a higher shift allowance for weekend working, but with no overtime. They didn't even need to work at weekends if the work was done within the week. The company got all of the work done without overtime.

The time off in lieu does not have to be a straight hour to hour ratio. It can be that overtime rates are applied to the hours. In exchange for working overtime in one period the company can give them more time off at another time. So, if they take their time off in accordance with the rules, they may take a 12-hour shift off on Monday when a manager can cover, but only 8 or 10-hours are added to the Bank. Hence, they are not penalized for taking time off in lieu instead of overtime. From the company point of view the cost is reduced. If they didn't need them to work, then they are not losing out and saving on overtime pay. From the employees' point of view, they are being paid not to work. Both parties win.

Time off in lieu does not need to be paid back immediately, so the Banked Hours can be rolled over and paid back in the following year.

Early Retirement

Some companies cannot recruit enough staff in a skill. This means that they are short. What's more they will continue to be short staffed indefinitely. However, this may not be acceptable because of legal or safety issues, so they over roster the people they have. This could mean that each year they will be faced with a large overtime bill.

So, one company came up with a different approach. Why not use Banked Hours? Banked Hours allowed them to keep track of the hours everyone worked, year after year. They just kept rolling the Banked Hours over. The plan is that when the shift workers are approaching retirement, they can use their Banked Hours. So the shift workers were looking at retiring three to six months early on full pay.

From the company's point of view, they were paying for the hours at basic rate and they wouldn't have to pay those hours for many years. They were hopeful that by the time their current shift workers retired, they would be able to find or train replacements. What's more it tied the shift workers to the company to an extent, because they had this opportunity of retiring early on full pay. If they left early they would still be paid, but it's not quite the same. A few weeks paid leave is not the same as retiring early. Not when you would be on the same pay for that time.

From the shift workers' point of view, they get to retire early on full pay. So, there would be no loss of earning for a few months before their pension kicked in. This was very attractive to them. After all what it amounted to was having to work two or three hours extra each week over the next ten years or so. The hours themselves were not arduous. The shift pattern was designed to limit fatigue, ensure that they had ample rest. It was like the equivalent to staying behind for an extra 15 minutes at the end of the shift.

Long Term Sickness

Banked hours were designed to cover for short term sickness and absence. Ideally long-term absence should be covered in another way. People on long term sick should not be on shift or on a night shift pattern anyway. This is because working nights disrupts their eating and sleeping patterns. When you are ill and taking medication, it is very important that your sleep and eating habits are regular. Otherwise it disrupts medication and impacts on the person's health and recovery.

Therefore, when someone falls seriously ill an alternative needs to be found. Normally this results in the person being moved to a days only pattern and a replacement being recruited. This takes time. The Banked Hours system is there to help bridge the gap for a limited time but not indefinitely.

When designing a Banked Hours system, often the management team will design it with a set amount of absence cover built in. This would ideally be the absence rate plus 25%. This will then cover for natural variations in the absence rate. However it would not cover for a long term sick absence. So it may be that the absence will be covered using Banked Hours for the first four weeks. After that the management team should have come up with an alternative solution. Moving someone in from another department, running short, moving the work, covering it with agency or management. This would cover the time until either the person returned to work or a replacement has been recruited and trained.

This four-week grace period is to ensure that there is no immediate effect to the work. There is time to think about alternative solutions and implement them. However, having the absence rate skewed for four weeks, because of one person's absence, will impact on some people more than others. This is because with a pattern, the same people, tend to cover for a person.

Hence in a four-week period, some people may go from a positive Bank of Hours to a negative Bank because they are covering the absent person's shifts. If this is a blip, because of a one off absence, and you have solved it at the end of four weeks, you can either chose to pay for the excess hours using overtime, or roll the Bank over into the next year.

After all, the nature of Banked Hours means that some years you will not use everyone's Banked Hours because the absence rate is lower than average. Other years you may have higher absence rates. For some the average Banked Hours is always positive at the end of the year. However, some people may be lucky and others unlucky. So, you roll the Banked Hours over and hope that those that were unlucky last year will be lucky this year and end up with zero Banked Hours.

Another exception is authorised leave. Leave like bereavement, or jury duty will be a one off and can be easily covered by Banked Hours. However, leave like TA (Territorial Army) will happen to the same person every year and for a considerable amount of time. This sort of leave can be covered by Banked Hours. However there needs to be arrangements in place that the pattern will ensure that every year the same group of people is not covering the people on TA leave. Or if there are multiple people who are part of the TA, that these people are spread out through all of the teams to mitigate the effect.

Forming a Ring

One of the greatest risks to any on call system is that people form a ring. This is when shift workers band together to defraud the company, they take it in turn to call in absent knowing that one of their mates will have to be called in to cover their absence. Then when they are on-call, their mate returns the favour and calls in sick so that they are brought in. This usually happens when overtime is involved.

However, rings can form whenever there is an option to gain additional payments. This can be to the company's benefit as well as to its detriment.

If people will be paid overtime if they use up all of their Banked Hours, then people may deliberately use up their Banked Hours, to be given money when they are called in. They may also do this so that they are taken off the on-call rota once they have met their quota of Banked Hours for the year.

This sort of behavior may be of benefit to the company. For one thing they are getting someone in to cover when they need it. However, if people are allowed to pick and choose when they can pay back their Banked Hours, they are all going to choose Monday to Friday Day shifts and not cover Friday and Saturday Night shifts.

If someone is using up all of their Banked Hours too quickly, then this needs to be investigated. The system is either faulty and not sharing out the Banked Hours evenly, or the person working the Banked Hours is trying to use them up, or someone else is taking advantage of them. Either way it needs investigating.

Example of forming a ring using 232 shift pattern. In this example two people on different teams have formed a ring. They call in sick when they know their counterpart will be on cover and have to come into to work.

Names	Hours Worked	Shifts Worked	Wed 01-Jan	Thu 02-Jan	Fri 03-Jan	Sat 04-Jan	Sun 05-Jan	Mon 06-Jan	Tue 07-Jan	Wed 08-Jan	Thu 09-Jan	Fri 10-Jan	Sat 11-Jan	Sun 12-Jan	Mon 13-Jan	Tue 14-Jan	Wed 15-Jan	Thu 16-Jan
P1	1690.5	175	C1	N	N	N				D	D		C2	C2	N	N		
P2	1690.5	173		D	N	N	N			D	D					N	SN	
P3	1690.5	175	C2		N	N	N			D	D	C1			N			
P4	1690.5	176			N	N	N			D	D		C1	C1	N			
P5	1690.5	174			N	N	N			D	D	C2			N			
P6	1702	176	D	SD		C2	C2	N	N		D	D	D			N	N	N
P7	1702	175	D	D				N	N		D	D	D	C2		N	N	N
P8	1702	176	D	D	C1			N	N		D	D	D		C2	N	N	N
P9	1702	176	D	D		C1	C1	N	N		D	D	D			N	N	N
P10	1702	176	D	D	C2			N	N		D	D	D	C1		N	N	N

Figure 17: Example of ring

Figure 17 shows the 232-shift pattern. P2 and P6 have formed a ring. When P2 was on cover, January 2nd, P6 called in sick so that P2, is called in to cover. Then on the 14th January, P2 returns the favour and calls in sick so that P6 is called in to cover.

Rings may be formed with many people and the swapping may take place over several months, therefore it is very hard to spot. If you find that a ring has been formed, then these people are subject to disciplinary procedures.

However, rings have formed to benefit the company. If the company offered a bonus scheme for attendance, where by anyone who does not call in sick during the year gets a bonus, then a ring can be formed to ensure that everyone receives the bonus.

If in the shift pattern above, where a ring was formed to defraud the company, we look at it as an opportunity to reduce absence. P6 is really sick. They look at the rota and see that P2 is going to be called in to cover. So, P6 calls up P2 and say, "I'm sick, you are going to have to cover for me. But how would you like to swap a shift. You work my Day shift on 2nd January, and I'll do the cover. Then in a month or so, we can do a reverse swap. I'll work a day shift and you can do my cover. That way I get to keep my attendance bonus." We have seen companies with no sickness!

Example of using Banked Hours

Every operation is different and every one needs it's own solution. There are often many solutions that you could employ.

Outline of the problem:

- An operation has flat staffing 24/7 currently using five teams of five with a team leader. 30 staff in total.
- 12h hour shifts 7am-7:30pm and 7pm-7:30am so there is a 30 minute handover and 30 minutes unpaid break
- Contracted working hours 37hpw and 35 days of holiday including Bank Holidays
- Currently on DDNN-4off holidays included option with 10-day breaks
- Currently of the 259h of holiday entitlement, 172 hours are incorporated into the pattern and 87h or 8 shifts, or golden days, can be taken at any time subject to holiday policy and procedures.
- Five days of training is required, 37h per year
- Absence is high at 6.5%
- They require a minimum of four on shift at all times
- They need extra people on days Monday-Friday standard opening hours as there is admin and other work that requires liaising with other departments on office hours
- Currently overtime is high and expensive
- Hiring additional person is not an option

So at the moment they have six people scheduled to work, 24/7 one of which is the team leader. The team leader can step down and cover if necessary however they have their own work to do and constantly covering is causing problems.

The holidays not included equate to 240 shifts per year. They can cope if one person per shift is on holiday as they drop down to four. Unfortunately they then have absences and training which cause further reductions and this often leads to them dropping below the 4 minimum threshold. In the year, there are 730 scheduled shifts, so there are 730 possible times to take the 240 shifts. The Summer is about 120 days, or 240 shifts, There are 52 weekends with 260 shifts if we count Friday Night as a weekend shift.

Holidays are mainly booked at weekends and during the summer and on the Night shift. Absences are random and there are about 310 shifts of absence. Training days take up about 150 shifts. So holidays, absences and training days take up about 700 shifts of the 730 available shifts

They are having to spend overtime on bringing extra people in Monday-Friday and they are having to bring people in on overtime when holidays coincide with absences.

To make matters worse they each have the option of purchasing up to five extra days of holiday or three extra shifts per year. Many of them exercise this option.

Solution

Handover and Staggered Starts

Firstly remove the handover. Instead of a 30-minute handover we use a 30 minute staggered start. This means that half the team come in at 7am and go home at 7pm. The other half come in at 7:30am and go home at 7:30pm. This means that half of the day shift is on for 30 minutes with half of the night shift. This allows them to pass on any information over what happened at night. The procedure was also changed to include a more detailed log book outlining any events from the previous shift. This allowed for the handover to be replaced with a staggered start. The same thing happened on the night shift.

In some situations a physical handover is necessary for example the crews need to change clothes before and after a shift or a machine needs constant monitoring and the arriving crew needs to take over at a convenient point.

If it is the passing over of information, as in this case, then overlapping shifts and new information processes can eliminate or minimise handover times.

The shift is now 11.5h paid instead of 12h paid.

Shift Pattern

Changing the shift pattern often changes people's lifestyle. Those who have worked the 4on-4off know how precious weekends are. The problem is that they often work six out of eight weekends, the six being consecutive weekends. It is better on the holidays included version but the fact that the pattern is an 8-day pattern and the week is seven days, means that you still get split weekends. A split weekend is where you are working either the Saturday or the Sunday but not both. This invariably means that you will work more weekends.

Many people on the 4on-4off prefer the 554 option. This is because you are adding an extra shift but the pattern now revolves around the weekends. So the number of weekends they are working reduces. On their current pattern you are looking at working on 26-31 weekends per year where they are working for the whole or part of the weekend. On the 554 holidays included shift pattern this drops to 21 weekends. A vast difference.

Banked Hours

If added to all this we also bring in Banked Hours then we start to build a robust solution.

So instead of five people on each shift, if we can cope with four let's go down to four. The fifth person's hours now go into the bank. These hours can be used to provide Monday-Friday shifts. In this example two people will be rostered onto working Monday-Friday and this rotates through everyone. (Note the extra Monday-Friday shifts are removed on Bank Holidays, and Christmas week). The Monday to Friday shifts are the standard 37-hour week and office hours.

The rest of the hours go into the Bank. This means that on average each person has 180 hours in the Bank. That 4,500 hours for the 25 people.

The Team Leads are different. As they can't be stood down, they don't have a Bank of Hours. On average they are owed 14 hours after holidays.

Everyone's standard 35 days of holiday is now all included in the shift pattern. 180h in the Bank can now cover for training and absence. There are not enough hours in the Bank to cover for the extra three shifts of holiday if they chose to purchase them. Therefore if these were covered it would have to be at overtime.

It's very important when using Bank Hours to know when to use them, how and for what purpose. In this case 4,500 hours would cover the 25x37h of training or 925hours per year. It would also cover the absences of ~3,100 hours per year. Thus at the end of the year each person would have about 18hours in the Bank that would be zeroed. These 18 hours are a reward for covering the absences and training but also as a buffer in case one person ended up working more than their Bank in any one year.

On average they would each gain 18hours to compensate them for the inconvenience of covering these events at short notice.

Holidays, absences, training are all covered. So then we need cover shift to ensure that they are able to come in when required. Cover shifts are there for the company because they have already built in a system to say who will come in when. This means that when an absence is reported, regardless of who takes the call, they can initiate the response.

From the shift workers point of view the cover shifts mean that they are only down to be brought in on their cover shifts. Without cover shifts, the employees would be always wondering which day are they going to be brought in.

Names	Hours Worked	Shifts Worked	Mon 01-Jan	Tue 02-Jan	Wed 03-Jan	Thu 04-Jan	Fri 05-Jan	Sat 06-Jan	Sun 07-Jan	Mon 08-Jan	Tue 09-Jan	Wed 10-Jan	Thu 11-Jan	Fri 12-Jan	Sat 13-Jan	Sun 14-Jan	Mon 15-Jan	Tue 16-Jan	Wed 17-Jan	Thu 18-Jan	Fri 19-Jan	Sat 20-Jan	Sun 21-Jan	Mon 22-Jan	Tue 23-Jan	Wed 24-Jan	Thu 25-Jan	Fri 26-Jan	Sat 27-Jan	Sun 28-Jan
Team A Lead	1713.5	149	D	D	N	N				D	D	N	N								D	D	D	N	N					
Team A P1	1493.5	166								D1	D1	N1	N1	N1			C2	C2			D	D	D	N	N					
Team A P2	1474.5	163	D	D	N	N															D	D	D	N	N		C2	C2		
Team A P3	1539.5	172	D	D	N	N	C1	C1	C1	D1	D1	N1	N1	N1																
Team A P4	1532	171	D1	D1	N1	N1	C2	C2	C2	D	D	N	N	N							D1	D1	D1	N1	N1					
Team A P5	1539.5	170	D1	D1	N1	N1				D	D	N	N	N			C1	C1			D1	D1	D1	N1	N1		C1	C1		
Team B Lead	1725	150			D	D	N	N	N			D	D	D	N	N														
Team B P1	1514	167			D1	D1	N1	N1	N1					C2	C2		D	D	D	N	N									
Team B P2	1486	164												D	D	D	N	N	C2	C2										
Team B P3	1456.5	161			C1		D1	D1	N1	N1	N1													M	M	M	M	F		
Team B P4	1551	171			C2		D	D	N	N	N					D1	D1	D1	N1	N1										
Team B P5	1543.5	171					D	D	N	N	N			C1	C1	D1	D1	D1	N1	N1	C1	C1		M	M	M	M	F		
Team C Lead	1667.5	145								D	D	D	N	N							D	D	N	N						
Team C P1	1456.5	162					C2	C2		D	D	D	N	N							D	D	N	N			C1	C1		
Team C P2	1493.5	167								D	D	D	N	N			C2	C2			D	D	N	N			C1	C1		
Team C P3	1414	157															M	M	M	M	F			D1	D1	N1	N1		C2	C2
Team C P4	1493.5	165								D1	D1	D1	N1	N1							D1	D1	N1	N1						
Team C P5	1508.5	171					C1	C1		D1	D1	D1	N1	N1			C1	C1						M	M	M	M	F		
Team D Lead	1656	144	N	N													D	D	N	N				D	D	N	N	N		
Team D P1	1475	163	N	N													D	D	N	N										
Team D P2	1482	166	N	N			C2	C2									D	D	N	N	C1	C1	C1	D1	D1	N1	N1	N1		
Team D P3	1459	162								M	M	M	M	F			D1	D1	N1	N1	C2	C2	C2	D	D	N	N	N		
Team D P4	1475	163	N1	N1													D1	D1	N1	N1				D	D	N	N	N		
Team D P5	1459	164	N1	N1			C1	C1		M	M	M	M	F										D1	D1	N1	N1	N1		
Team E Lead	1656	144								D	D	N	N								D	D	N	N	N				D	D
Team E P1	1482	164								D	D	N	N								D	D	N	N					D	D
Team E P2	1482	167								D	D	N	N	C1	C1	C1					D1	D1	N1	N1	N1					
Team E P3	1504	170					M	M	F	D1	D1	N1	N1	C2	C2	C2					D	D	N	N	N			D1	D1	D1
Team E P4	1482	164								D1	D1	N1	N1								D	D	N	N	N	C1	C1	D1	D1	D1
Team E P5	1458	163					M	M	F												D1	D1	N1	N1	N1	C2	C2	D	D	D

Figure 18: Staggered starts, 554 with cover shifts and weekday shifts

Figure 18 shows what the shift pattern would look like. They are all working a different number of hours over the year. This is because the pattern is a five week pattern for the Team Leaders. It's a 25 week rotation for the team members and then they have their Bank Holiday shifts removed if they are down to work weekday shifts.

Figure 17 shows the number on shift for the shift pattern shown in figure 16. There are two different 12-hour day shifts D and D1. The D1 shift starts half an hour later than the D shift. This means that two of the people from the night shift will still be on duty between 7 and 7:30am. So if there is any information to handover about events that took place over night, they are there to inform the day crew and answer any questions they might have.

There are two cover shifts on each day: C1 and C2. If an absence occurs then C1 is down to cover. If two absences occur C1 and C2 would be called in. Numbering the cover shifts means that the person calling them in doesn't need to make a decision as to who to call in. It also means that it is fair, each person stands just as much chance of being called in as anyone else. The hours they work come out of their banked hours.

	Start Time	Finish Time	Monday	Tuesday	Wednesday	Thursday	Friday	Saturday	Sunday	Monday	Tuesday	Wednesday	Thursday	Friday	Saturday	Sunday	Monday	Tuesday	Wednesday	Thursday	Friday	Saturday	Sunday
D	07:00	19:00	3	3	3	3	3	3	3	3	3	3	3	3	3	3	3	3	3	3	3	3	3
N	19:00	07:00	3	3	3	3	3	3	3	3	3	3	3	3	3	3	3	3	3	3	3	3	3
D1	07:30	19:30	2	2	2	2	2	2	2	2	2	2	2	2	2	2	2	2	2	2	2	2	2
N1	19:30	07:30	2	2	2	2	2	2	2	2	2	2	2	2	2	2	2	2	2	2	2	2	2
C1	07:00	07:00	1	1	1	1	1	1	1	1	1	1	1	1	1	1	1	1	1	1	1	1	1
M	08:30	17:00			2	2				2	2	2	2				2	2	2	2			
C2	07:00	07:00	1	1	1	1	1	1	1	1	1	1	1	1	1	1	1	1	1	1	1	1	1
F	08:30	16:30					2							2							2		
Total			12	12	14	14	14	12	12	14	14	14	14	14	12	12	14	14	14	14	14	12	12

Figure 19: Shifts table for the example shift pattern

Monday to Thursday there are two M shifts or 8:30-5pm scheduled. On Friday they have an early finish so go home at 4:30pm, this shift is called F for Friday. The two on M shifts perform the admin work and liaison with other departments

You will note that the M shift is absent on the first Monday and Tuesday. This is because Monday is 1st Jan 2024 in this example. So the weekday shift has been dropped from the 1st and 2nd of January. However the 24/7 operation is still fully staffed.

Holidays

All of the holidays are incorporated into the shift pattern. The year is 52.14 weeks and the shift patterns are 5 weeks and 15 weeks for their rotation. This means that in any given year they will not work the average but the shift pattern will oscillate around the average. The same goes for the holidays each person gets. On average the team Leads would get 10.4 12-day breaks each. That is a 12-day break every five weeks. In figure 18 you can see that Team Lead E is off in week 1. In week 2, Team Lead D is off. In week three Team Lead C is off, and so on for the whole year. Each week a Team Leader is rostered off for 12-days.

The Team Members have a 25 week rotation. So during the 25 weeks they are rostered off for 3 12-day breaks at the same time as the Team Leader. However two of the Team Members are scheduled to work a week of weekday shifts. M shift Monday to Thursday and an F shift on Friday.

However in each block of shifts, one member of the team is rostered off. In week 1 in figure 18 you can see Team A P1 is rostered off when the rest of their team is scheduled to work DDNN.

This means they also get an 11-day break and two 14-day breaks every 25 weeks. So over the year they get:

- 2 x 11-day breaks
- 6 x 12-day breaks
- 4 x 14-day breaks

Effectively they get one long break each month.

Shifts

The Team Leads are scheduled to work on 146.4 shifts per year on average or 1,683.6 hours per year. They get ~218 days off per year. This means that on average they are working two shifts too many. Thus either they are paid overtime for these two shifts, or they have them as Golden Days and can take them within the rules during the year.

The team members are scheduled to work on 136 days on average, are on call for 30 days and off for 199 days.

The probability of them being called in on a C1 shift is 55% for absence cover. They also have to cover training too, but this will be known a long time in advance. The probability of them being called in on a C2 shift is 18% for absence cover.

If more than two people are absent on any day, then the Team Leads would help cover as would the weekday people if it happened Monday-Friday. This may happen a few times per year.

Managers

The great thing about this sort of operation is that all of the hard work and decisions have been made in advance for the smooth running of the operation. This means that a manager comes into work and doesn't need to focus on managing the holidays or providing cover. The work has already been done.

The manager doesn't need to rearrange the work each shift because five turned up today and four turned up tomorrow and three turned up the day after. Every day is the same. Thus it reduces their stress, it reduces their planning and it reduces the uncertainty. So if they are asked, when a piece of work will be finished, they can guarantee it. This is because they will always have the correct number available come holidays, sickness, training and all the usual uncertainties managers have to deal with.

Instead the manager can focus on making more money, reducing bottlenecks, creating a better product.

Summary

This solution is about using multiple flexible working techniques. The staggered starts are designed to reduce the need for a handover. The Banked Hours are there to cover for training and absence. The holidays included is about reducing the uncertainty. Shift swaps would be allowed to ensure that people could have the time off that they wanted and with a long break almost every month they have lots of opportunity to arrange their own agenda. There is also Overtime to cover for the optional holidays and to cover the Team Leads, they also Step Down when needed. There is also variable shift length, Monday-Friday we don't need extra people on for the full 12-hours, so we employ reduced shift lengths.

It is quite normal to use more than one technique to solve the different problems. This solution is a low cost solution. It increases productivity and creates a nice work/life balance for the teams. The result is continuity and stability.

From the clients perspective, this operation will always be fully staffed and have the extra resources on during the week to interact with other departments. The team members always know that they will not be overworked, as they will always have a full compliment on every shift. This creates a constant and minimal stress environment. In comparison to previously when they didn't know how many would be coming in on the shift. If there is only work for four people and five turn up, what does the fifth person do? A manager doesn't like to see a person sat doing nothing, and neither do the other people or the poor person is sat in a corner bored to tears. Therefore the operation has to be reorganised to accommodate them. This is not only inefficient because it costs 25% extra manpower, but also results in less work being completed because everyone is being shuffled around to give them equal work. Then on the Day shift Monday to Friday, they either have too few people than needed or they are reshuffled at the end and beginning of the shift.

Managers now have the perfect alignment of skills and staffing numbers on each and every shift. They don't have to worry about holidays, absences or training effecting the operation. This means that they can plan accurately, well into the future. If managers do run into any problems, they can focus on solving it and then implementing best practice as they are not busy trying to firefight a continually changing operation and creating multiple solutions depending on the staffing levels that day or that shift. The solution also allows for the optimal solution at the lowest possible cost while increasing productivity.

The team members now have certainty when they come into work, they know what they will be doing and also who else and the number of people who will be working with them. This gives them consistency and makes their working conditions easy. The Team Lead has no decisions to make as regards covering for absences, or how to juggle five people to do the work of four, or worse, four people to do the work of six. The team members know when they have to work, when they are off and the dates they may have to work, so there is minimum contact by work outside of work. They are not bothered by calls asking if they can work that day. Everything is organized months ahead.

All of the team members know that everything will be fair. There is no discrimination. Everyone who has the same skills is treated the same, down to when they are asked to work as the covers are numbered, it is down to fate not the manager to chose who will work when. They all get equal shift allowance as they all work the same unsocial shifts. They get the same chance of being called in to cover using up their Bank Hours. They get the same days off.

It means that they have control of their lives. Their private lives are their own. They don't have to ask the manager if they can have this week off because it's their cousin's wedding. They don't have to ask the manager if they can go home early because their child is in the school play. If they are working on a special day then they can arrange a swap to ensure they get the time off they want.

The work becomes routine and easy. It's about minimising stress and maximising potential. And if everything goes to plan and they are not called in to work all of their Banked Hours, they get extra paid time off.

If they were office staff they would be scheduled to work 260 days per year and have seven weeks off of holiday. On this operation they work on around 136 days and are on cover for another 30 with 199 days off. To put this into perspective that's about 50% more days off than office staff equivalent.

When they were on all 12-hour shifts, they were scheduled for 146 shifts, so the 136 is an improvement there too. Instead of the 12 10-day breaks they get on the 4on-4off with 10-day breaks, they now get the same number of long breaks but they are all of a longer duration. The only thing they are losing out on is the overtime earnings they are currently enjoying. What they gain is consistency and predictability.

They also work 14 fewer nights each year and 4 fewer weekend shifts each year.

The ability to organise your own shift pattern is very important to the individual. Being able to swap shifts is how they can arrange which days they work and which days they don't work. They have the autonomy to set up which weeks off they get as well as individual shifts.

Matching Capacity to Demand

Businesses need to be able to respond to market demand faster than ever before. Demand is getting harder to predict and organisations, be they businesses, hospitals or public bodies, need to be able to respond quickly and efficiently. If a business does not respond quickly, they lose the order. If a business does not respond efficiently, they lose money. If a business does not respond they will go out of business.

If a hospital does not respond to new demand as the population increases, patients will go untreated and some will die unnecessarily.

If a public body, be it a council or government department does not respond, the public will lose confidence in the authority. This will result with it being voted out of office, or worse go to the newspapers.

Getting the right people in the right place at the right time, and being able to change the staffing quickly depends on many factors. Being able to predict demand is one such factor. Being able to react to the demand is much more difficult. If the demand is variable and uncertain, the planned response must be variable and cover each element of uncertainty. This will involve short and long term planning.

The traditional solution is to use overtime and temporary labour to cover fluctuations in demand. In many situations this response is adequate and a 'pool' of workers are on stand-by. There is a finite level of extra capacity this can deliver in any given situation and there are many hidden drawbacks to relying on using overtime and temps.

The overtime tends to become institutionalized and abused. It becomes a fixed cost rather than a flexible cost. Some shifts are more popular than others. If you are paid the same for working overtime on a Monday day as on a Friday night, covering the Friday night is difficult. Working overtime in February is very different to during the Summer. So when overtime is abundant, it becomes hard to cover the unsocial shifts.

Temps need training and the constant need for training and retraining as technology changes makes them very expensive.

Multi-Strategy solutions require IT methods and resources. Flexible working that meets the flexible workload requires a variable planned response where all the elements of using labour are utilised. Having a pool of multi-skilled and specialist, full-time workers, part-time workers, annualised hours to vary the working week, overtime and temporary labour on variable contracts, are all used to expand and contract capacity to meet the demand curve.

A report on official statistics shows that nearly 10% of all UK employees working for less than 45 hours per week, would like to work more hours. This figure only reflects those who want to work at basic rates and excludes the sizeable number who would work at overtime rates. This means that you could get more work out of your employees without having to pay them a premium. The statistics also revealed that more part-time than full-time employees wanted longer hours. And of this group, those in the 35-49 age group wanted longer hours the most. This is ideal if you are looking to increase production or provide a greater range of services - by considering part-timers first, you are less likely to have to pay overtime and won't have to worry about exceeding the 48 hours per week limit.

Inventory Modeling

Inventory modeling is of interest to all organisations. Companies have huge amounts of capital tied up in stock so it's important to ensure you have the correct amount of stock.

There are six reasons for having stock:

1. Cycle stock: This is where you order stock and hold it as it goes out at a steady or variable rate
2. Congestion stock: If you have large batch sizes and multiple products produced on the same lines then you will need to hold stock for when the line is producing the other products
3. Buffer stock: When either the demand or supply is variable you will need to hold stock to have faster customer response time
4. Pipeline stock: This is stock being transported to the customer
5. Anticipation stock: Where the costs of raw materials is likely to rise, you may want to stock up when the price is low

6. Decoupling stock: This is where stock is held in different locations to allow decentralised decision making

When modeling your inventory it is important to understand why you are holding the stock and the cost of that stock. Then you can make important decisions like: should you minimise stock or maximise customer response times.

If you can vary your capacity you can potentially reduce your buffer stock, as you can respond quicker to changes in demand. It may also depend on the size and cost of storing the raw ingredients compared to the final product. If it is cheaper to store the raw ingredients, then you want to match your output to demand as closely as possible. If on the other hand there is a long shelf life, the product is smaller and cheaper to store than the ingredients, you might want to match your output to supply. This means that you store the raw materials for the shortest length of time possible.

Our clients, for example, often need to supply bulk products in small packets and this affects the way they schedule their employees. Apples, potatoes and most foods grow as bulk products and are dispensed continuously in small packets of apple pie, frozen chips and bread. LNG and oil arrives in bulk and is dispensed as a continuous stream of gas and petrol. Dock workers can only load and unload ships when they are in habour, not when they are at sea. Paint, heating oil and Christmas puddings are seasonal products. Rain water is seasonal but waste water is a continuous steady stream. Then the two largest seasonal on/off industries of education and tourism. If you had flat staffing as the only available resource, you would find it much more expensive than variable staffing.

Abuses of Banked Hours

Banked Hours work for the shift worker and the company provided they are not abused. Once Banked Hours are in place they are there forever. The only time we have been asked to take them out of the operation, is because individual managers have abused them.

Some managers feel that people are being paid to be *in* work. Therefore, they should be in work. If there is no genuine work for them to do, they make things up. They force them to sweep the yard, clean the cars etc. While that may be genuine work, it should not be a punishment and definitely, should not, be a way of using up Banked Hours.

Banked Hours are part of a service. The employee is being paid to work at certain times and to be available *if and only if* needed at others. They are being paid to provide a service, a very necessary service. A service that makes the company more efficient.

Therefore, it is important to list the reasons when and why banked hours should be used. This list should be used when estimating the number of Banked Hours required for the operation. There should also be some additional hours put into the Bank to cover for annual variations. Then some hours should be added as an incentive for the scheme.

When people are then asked to come in to work their Banked Hours, it needs to be for one of the genuine reasons e.g. training, cover for absent colleagues, ad-hoc work, meetings, etc. The only punishment use of Banked Hours is disciplinary meetings.

If the yard does need to be swept and cars washed, then it should be a regular job. People should not lose their Banked Hours to menial jobs created by petty managers that do not understand the value of their shift workers.

Banked Hours is a privilege. It should be seen by the shift workers as a bonus. It should be seen by managers as a tool for covering genuine work.

Abuses of Banked Hours by Shift Workers

Banked Hours is a privilege. People are being paid to provide a service. If they fail to provide the service, then they need to have their privileges revoked and be subject to other disciplinary procedures.

So, if they refuse or fail to come into work on a cover shift, this should be treated in the same way as missing a normal shift.

If they do not turn up on time or in an appropriate condition (provided they were given enough notice) on their cover shift, then they are subject to the same disciplinary procedure as if they did this on a normal shift. We recommend that the person on the previous shift cannot leave until relieved by their manager or the person coming to work the next shift.

If they create a ring, then they need to be taken off Banked Hours and be the subject of disciplinary procedures.

The Banked Hours system runs on trust. People can swap shifts and cover shifts. However, they may abuse this trust if they bully colleagues into swapping shifts so that they always have the Friday or Saturday night off. This is where the shift allowance comes in. People are paid a shift allowance to work unsociable hours. If they do not work their quota of unsociable hours, then they need to have this payment stopped or reduced. This is why all swaps must have management approval. Also all managers must monitor and check to see that the system or a person is not abused.

Another common abuse is to swap all their covers for later in the year and then leave. This forces their colleagues to work more covers. An easy way to manage this is to divide the year into quarters. Everyone needs to work a minimum number of shifts and covers in each quarter.

The biggest abuse is when the system is started on an honours system. As Banked Hours relies on mutual trust, then often the case is made that there is no need for an official rota made out for the cover arrangement. That, when needed, a volunteer will come forward. Then people refuse to come in when required. They turn off their mobiles. Fail to pick up messages. They claim they didn't know the company needed them. Then the manager has to come in and work in their stead.

There needs to be a disciplinary procedure for this. We recommend that within each year, if a person fails to come in once during the year, stating they didn't know they were needed. It is a genuine mistake. If it happens a second time, then they are subject to disciplinary procedure. If it happens a third time they are taken off the Banked Hours system. The usual reaction to the failing of the honours method is that all privileges are removed, and people are scheduled to work all their contracted hours. This can often mean the removal of any extra allowances, the purchasing of additional hours is stopped, holidays are rationed, and quotas imposed, Golden Days are revoked, shift swaps are not allowed, absences are scrutinised closely, rules are followed, etc. This is because the trust between employees and managers has gone and managers feel betrayed.

Fears by Shift Workers

Some managers feel that once a person is on the Banked Hours system, then they are available to come into work, whenever they are required. They are effectively on call 24/7. Just like a soldier, they are always on alert. They must obey or be accused of dereliction of duty.

Work is not a battle field. Even soldiers are given leave when they are not subject to being called to duty. People need a work/life balance. They need to know when they will be required to work and when they can relax away from work. That is where the cover shifts help.

People feel they have the right to know in advance; when they will be working, when they may be working and when they will definitely not be working.

Some shift workers fear that the manager will always be picking on them, possibly due to past experiences. That they will always be the one who is asked to come in and work. That every Saturday they are down to cover will result in them being called in on the Saturday Night at no notice. This is not fair. It's not fair to the employee if it happens and it's not fair to the Manager if it's not happening.

This perception can arise as follows. When an employee is not on shift and is not called in to cover an absence, they have no idea of what is happening elsewhere in the organisation. There can have been multiple absences and frantic cover arrangements going on for days without them being in the slightest way bothered by it. That is the whole point of these arrangements, that no one is bothered except by prior arrangement. Then they get the call to come in. How can they know if this is the first absence cover call-in for weeks, or the 50th that week? The system says not to bother a person until they are needed, so they aren't contacted. The fact that they are continually being bothered on the days they have arranged to cover, is precisely the purpose of the system. When they talk about this later on, what they find is that they were the only person contacted and no one else knew anything about it. Again, that is precisely what should happen, but it can feel all wrong. If they are used to their previous system of the manager phoning everyone up on a round robin, trying to persuade people to come in, this can feel very alien, and the first reaction is that of 'bias'.

That is why we recommend numbering the cover shifts and calling people as soon as you know they might be needed or definitely will be needed. Often this can be months ahead. Then the manager cannot be accused of manipulating the system and making one person work more Banked Hours than another. If the shift pattern is fair, then it is the luck of the draw as to who is asked to come and who gets more time off. It is not the manager dictating the operation.

Incidentally, we have analysed many sickness records to find patterns of sickness. It helps if you can do an analysis on your records, but the statistics can be quite onerous to extract. There is some difference between 12-hour shifts and 8-hour shifts, but these are the following findings.

Every sickness has a 1st day of sickness, obvious I know but it is an important factor in the analysis, however it is rare that a person is sick for only one day. Hence most sickness occurs on the 2nd and subsequent days of absence. What this means is that most sick days, and their cover, is known 24 hours or more ahead of time. So if there are 350 occasions of sickness involving 850 days, then 500 days are classed as the 2nd and subsequent days. This is an important parameter in the analysis.

Let's take an example of sickness over a year from two different sources. Table 6 shows the absence statistics of two facilities. They were both using the 4on-4off shift pattern with 12-hour shifts. Therefore, the results are comparable. The shift pattern often leads to a sickness pattern. Both these facilities were of a similar size and had about 120 employees on shift. Neither of these facilities had a cover system and absences are covered by having extra people on shift or by call-in on overtime.

Table 6: Comparison of Length of Absence for two Facilities

Absence (days)	Facility 1 occasions	Facility 1 days off	Facility 2 occasions	Facility 2 days off
½ DAY	7	3.5	4	2
1 DAY	91	91	117	117
2 DAYS	89	178	130	260
3 DAYS	62	186	40	120
4 DAYS	80	320	59	236
5 DAYS	3	15	2	10
6 DAYS	0	0	2	12
7 DAYS	4	28	0	0
10 DAYS	1	10	0	0
12 DAYS	2	24	0	0
TOTAL	339	855.5	354	757

This table refers to shifts as days. It is based on the 4on-4off shift pattern, so for instance 5 days would be an illness that spans over two lots of the sets of 4 shifts. So it might 3 shifts in one set, then 4 days off, then 2 shifts in the following set of 4 shifts.

Assuming that the absence statistics remained the same and everyone was on a cover arrangement, then in Facility 1, the 120 employees would have been called in on 339 occasions at short notice on the first day of each absence period. That is about three times a year each. There are 14 shifts in the week, seven Day shifts and seven Night shifts, but there is only one Saturday Night shift in the week.

Let's consider what would have happened if instead of covering through extra staff on duty these facilities had used Cover shifts and Banked Hours. Their absence rate was about 4% depending on how you calculate it. Here we have 120 employees scheduled to 182 shifts per year and we had 855 shifts of absence, which is 4%. There are about 30 on duty before holidays and absence. Statistical analysis shows that this means that there could be up to six missing off a shift due to sickness.

Table 7: Statistical Probability of Absence on Shift

Probability of Absence on Shift   Number of Occasions

No. of Absences	Probability	One Year	Five Years	10 Years
0	0.2939	215	1073	2145
1	0.3673	268	1341	2681
2	0.2219	162	810	1620
3	0.0863	63	315	630
4	0.0243	18	89	177
5	0.0053	4	19	28
6	0.0009	1	3	7
7	0.0001	0	0	1

The table 7 shows how many shifts had how many absences if we have a 4% absence rate and 30 employees on every shift. The first column is the number of absences per shift. The second column is the probability of that many people being absent. Therefore on any given shift there is a 29% probability of no one being absent on shift. The operation has 730 shifts of 12 hours, and on 215 shifts in the year, we expect no one will be absent. On 268 shifts there will be one absence, and so on.

This sort of analysis means that you can make important decisions. For instance if you have one person on cover, how often during the year will you be running short? Then you can compare the cost of having people on call and available to cover for an absence against the loss of business/production of running short.

The number of cover shifts used should reflect the amount of absence predicted on each shift, 6 in this case. In practice you might not go for six cover shifts per shift or 12 cover shifts per day, as the chance of six people being absent from one shift is very low. Instead you might go for five per day to cover both Day and Night shifts and run short on the couple of days per year when you have more than five absences. You can do a manual check for your organisation to verify your figures.

So, if you had five on absence cover per day, each of the 120 shift workers would be on cover about 15 times per year.

So, let's consider what would happen to an employee (John) who is on this shift pattern and cover rota. Well he is down to cover on about 15 days per year. 15 days per year spread evenly throughout the week means that he is down to cover about two Mondays, two Tuesdays, two Wednesdays, two Thursdays, two Fridays, two Saturdays and two Sundays.

Then let's consider how likely he is to be called in at short notice. Well for both facilities there were about 350 separate occasions of sickness. Facility one has 339 lots of sickness varying in length from ½ a shift to 12 shifts. Facility two has 354 lots of sickness varying in length from ½ a shift to 6 shifts. So, on average each day of the year will have one lot of short notice sickness. There are five people on cover, so John will only be called in to cover sickness at short notice on a fifth of his cover days. That is about three times per year. The probability that John is on cover and would be likely to be called in on a Saturday Night at short notice is just once in 5 years. Nowhere near as often as people imagine it will happen.

Of the 15 days when John is down to cover, he is likely to be called in about six of those cover days. On the rest of the cover shifts he will not be needed and can have a day off. So assuming that the absences are evenly spread across all of the shifts, John will be called in to work a cover on Saturday once a year. He will be called in to work a cover on Saturday Night about once every two years.

What John needs to remember is that he would be scheduled to work on 26 Saturday Nights in the 2 years, and on every one of those 26 occasions, the cover arrangement will guarantee they will have a full complement of staff and skills on shift, thus making the work that much easier. On those 26 occasions, everyone else who was either scheduled to work or down to cover came in to help John, so it seems only fair that John helps out on one occasion. To put it another way, in 5 years, John will be scheduled to work fully staffed up on 130 Saturday Nights if he provides short notice cover once. He will know about his cover shift a long time ahead, and in practice, the call-in on a Saturday will never be 'last minute'.

Sickness Statistics

Sickness is most often 2 days on 12-hour shifts or 3 days on 8-hour shifts. By most often, we mean there are more occasions of 2 days off than 1 day, 3 days, 4 days and so on.

There is more absence on a weekend day than a weekday day, for instance there is more absence on a Saturday than on a Wednesday. We put this down to the lack of medical services they can use on weekends, for instance their GP or pharmacy.

The shift pattern often affects the length of the absence. This is because if you are down to work four shifts and then off for four (4on-4off), there is a lot of illnesses which will last a week; colds, sprains. Therefore, a lot of sickness is for up to four shifts. Table 6 also shows that most of the absences are for two days. Illnesses like stomach upset, generally last for about two days. Then they often fall ill part way through a set of shifts meaning they are off sick for just one day whilst being sick for 2 days.

Looking at Table 6, and knowing both facilities are on a 4on-4off shift pattern, there is an obvious 'cliff-face' at 4 shifts of absence. Hardly any absences were for 5 days or more where '5 days' equates to 9 days of sickness. You can verify this phenomena in your organisation. The corollary of this is that a different shift pattern could well cause the absence rate to be different, either lower or higher depending on the number of consecutive working days and days off between sets of shifts.

Additional Payments

In a formal arrangement the cover will need to be paid for, since you are asking the staff to be on-call when they would normally be off.

Payments in Advance

There is often an On-Call, or Standby, payment. Typically, a yearly sum is agreed and paid monthly. If all staff are expected to be equally on-call, then all staff receive the same amount. Sometimes this is a percentage of their pay, more often it is a 'lump sum' as this divides up better. If a proportion of the staff are on-call, then they receive the pro-rata on-call payment.

For example, you want to have one person on-call 24/7 and you chose to have an on-call allowance of £10,000. If you have 20 people on the rota, with one person on-call each day to cover a 24-hour period. Then each person would receive £500 and be on call for about 18 days per year. That is £28 per day for being available. If only half the people volunteered, then there would only be 10 people on the on-call rota, then the on-call allowance would still be £10,000. Each person would then receive £1,000 but would be on-call for about 36 days per year. So, they would still receive £28 per day for being on-call.

Banked Hours Payments

Instead of an on-call payment, some companies use a Banked Hours arrangement. With Banked Hours they are paid in advance for hours that at some point they will be asked to work. The on-call or cover rota is there for the employees, so that they do not feel like they need to come in everyday, they would only be asked to come in on a few days per year. So the cover rota is part and parcel of the Banked Hours system. However if not all of the Banked Hours are used in a year, then they are discarded at the end of the year. So people are paid for hours that they never work.

This is instead of an on-call payment, or as well.

Overtime Payments

If people are being paid overtime to come in, this will often be enough of an incentive to be on the on-call rota without additional payments.

This depends on the probability of payment and the length of notice. So if you are covering for events weeks or even months in advance, then there is very little disruption to the individual and just overtime payment for the work might well be enough.

However if they are expected to put their life on hold when on-call and this continues through the on-call day, they may well expect additional payments.

If a person is rostered to cover 36 days per year, and the probability of coming in is only once or twice, they may feel that they need an additional payment for the inconvenience of being on-call but not being paid overtime for coming in. When you consider that if they are on-call then they will be expected to be available to come in and have made arrangements, this is not unreasonable.

Another way of paying for on-call, could be to use a daily rate rather than an annual rate. This could be linked to the cost of one hour's pay per day if they are not called out. This can be applied with Banked Hours so one hour is taken from their Bank for everyday they have to be available but are not used. This may or may not be at overtime rates.

TOIL – Time Off In Lieu

There doesn't have to be payment for the on-call rota. Instead people receive TOIL.

This takes the form of; all additional hours worked can be taken off at another time by mutual agreement. Usually this is at single time. It occurs after the hours are worked. Sometimes, this time is banked and taken as a block of time off.

There are often rules about what time can be taken off and within what time period. As a long-term example, one company allows staff to bank TOIL in their last 5 years of employment and take an earlier retirement.

For example, if each person was called in for about four 12-shifts per year, then in the last five years they could accumulate about

250 hours. This would mean retiring several months earlier on full pay.

They could also receive one-hour of TOIL if they are on-call but not called in to work. This may only be if they are expected to come in at short notice.

Cancelling On-Calls

If people only get on-call payments for short notice call-ins because of the disruption to their lives, then you could cancel the on-calls as the day approaches.

For example if we have 5 people on-call each day. You can estimate the probabilities for coming in for each person. As the day approaches, maybe only 1 on-call has been activated because of long term sick or training. The chances of the other four people coming in to cover for sickness reduces the closer you get to the day. So maybe a couple of days before the on-call shifts, you can cancel on-calls for two of them.

There can also be a cut off point. At the start of the night shift the previous day, if there has been no notice of sickness and no other reason for the on-call (weather, training, add-hoc workload, etc.) then they can be stood down.

Or the call-out might be within one-hour of the shift starting and if someone falls ill on shift, you manage it and not bring someone in specially.

Overnight On-Call

When work is mainly during the day, there is very little reason for a night shift. Therefore you have an on-call system instead in case of emergencies. Often this will be someone who is working that day. If an emergency occurs, the on-call is activated and they are sent to deal with the emergency. This can be in the office, remotely or out in the field.

As the person is working that day, there is very little inconvenience to being on-call overnight. Therefore they often have just an overtime payment. However since the person is being woken up, they need to be compensated.

This is sometimes a minimum length of call out. So even if it only takes them 30 minutes to deal with the emergency, they need to be compensated for being woken, getting dressed, making arrangements so that they can leave the house if they have children etc. So a minimum 3-hour call out is quite common. Also because they have lost sleep, if they are expected in the next day then they need compensating rest. They should have 11-hours between shifts, this is to ensure adequate rest. So they may come in 11-hours after they finish. Thus having a shorter shift the next day. Or they might start early. If the job finishes at 5am and they are expected back at 8am, they might as well stay on after 5am and work and then finish early.

If they don't have compensating rest because being on-call is always followed by a day off to minimise disruption on shift, then you might want to give a payment for the inconvenience of being called out.

Shift Allowance

When working shifts, there is often a shift allowance for unsociable shifts. Unsociable shifts are Lates, Nights, and weekend shifts. The more unsociable the shifts, the higher the payment.

If you use Banked Hours then there are less shifts overall and therefore pro-rata less unsociable shifts. On the face of it, this is a very good thing, why work extra nights and weekends if you don't have to? However if this results in reducing their shift allowance, this can have consequences.

Is it fair to get the same payment if you end up working more nights or weekends because of when you are asked to come in and cover?

What happens if you have to remain sober on Friday night because you are on-call and might have to work? Or you can't go away at the weekend because you are on-call?

In order to compensate for this, if people are asked to cover a lot of unsocial shifts, they might have their Bank reduced to compensate. So they have one-hour taken off their Bank for each weekend shift they are on-call.

Or the on-call shifts are taken into account when the shift allowance is calculated. They might only be worth half or a third of a real shift. Or if they do work a night maybe the hours are multiplied by the shift allowance. For instance if they work a 12-hour night, then 16 hours are taken off their Bank to show the unsociability of the shift they have covered.

Attendance Allowance

We can't get rid of sickness. However we can mitigate it if the procedures are in place. If a Banked Hours or cover system is in operation then people don't have to take a day off as sick. Instead they could swap a shift for a cover shift. This means that sickness levels would fall. This is desirable for the company and the other people on shift.

The person coming in to cover gets a day off as there would be an equivalent swap back at a later date. The other people on shift have a complete complement so they are not over worked. The sick person doesn't have to worry about seeing a doctor for a sick note or letting down their colleagues.

To encourage this behavior, because it is more efficient, there could be an attendance allowance. If there is no sickness each quarter or each year, then the individual gets a payment or bonus. This could be paid at Christmas or just before the summer holidays to help with costs at these times.

Union Negotiations

If you are a union official, then you will want Banked Hours for your members. Banked Hours help improve the work/life balance of your members, they reduce stress and give people more time off. So, they are a good thing to bring in.

However, you need to consider your members needs when negotiating for Banked Hours. We have assisted in many union negotiations as an independent third party. We were there to ensure that both the company and the shift workers got a good shift pattern that delivered for the company and gave a good work/life balance for the shift workers. You need a shift operation that works for all.

When you bring in Banked Hours there are several key points you need to discuss and agree upon in order to make a workable system. What you want is a win-win for both your members and the company. So, there are several things that you can both compromise on and several things that you shouldn't.

If your ONLY viewpoint is that it is an inconvenience to the cover person to be called in to work at short notice, then you have ignored all the benefits it brings to the employees. These include: paid time off, less stress, easier work, not being overworked, higher pay, training opportunities, shift swaps.

First things first: Why do you need Banked Hours?

When you are bringing in any new way of working, you need to ensure that everyone understands why it should be brought in. This comes down to the uses of Banked Hours. Are they to be used for training, ad-hoc work, sickness and absence cover etc.

Everyone needs to be very clear on what the intended uses and goals of the Banked Hours scheme are.

This is not a point to be negotiated, it is a key parameter that is the driving force behind the negotiations. During the negotiations you need to keep going back to the list and ensure that what you are agreeing to will deliver. Otherwise neither yourselves, your members or the company will be getting a workable system.

How many Banked Hours are Required?

This is what you need to negotiate. The company will want to give the shift workers the minimum number of hours to achieve its aims. However, as a union negotiator you will want some reward for your members. There are several ways to achieve this depending on the trust between your members and the managers. If you trust each other then you just need to include a margin to cover for all eventualities. For example, you work out how many hours are needed for the intended purposes e.g. 100 hours per year. Then you add on say 10% (about 10-hours) as a bonus for your members for working the scheme or to cover for fluctuations.

If there is little trust between management and your members, then instead of just negotiating a percentage you might negotiate a bonus scheme. So, on an on-call system you request that for every shift they are on-call but not called in, they get 1-hour deducted from their bank for being available. Or when they are called in they get paid not for the hours that they are called in for, but for 13-hours instead of 12.

The trust system assumes that at the end of the year all of the shift workers will have their Banked Hours zeroed and will have about 10% left as they were not needed. This is a bonus for ensuring the system worked. When you negotiate additional hours for being on-call, then you assume that there will be no hours in the Bank at the end of the year.

Purchasing Banked Hours

Sometimes more Banked Hours are needed than can be supplied by the contracted hours. The company would like to purchase these hours at basic rate. You would like the company to purchase these hours at overtime rates because they are additional hours.

This requires a comprise.

But what happens if a person uses up all of their Banked Hours and then is asked to come in and work more hours? Are these hours to be paid at overtime rate? And what overtime rate should be used?

End of Year Calculations

At the end of the year, your members will have worked a certain number of shifts, they will have been available for a certain number of days and they will have a number of Banked Hours in the Bank. What will happen to these hours?

Under normal circumstances the company would zero these hours. After all, if they didn't need them because the system worked, why will they need them next year?

However, many shift patterns roll over the year end. If you negotiated for on-call allowances with the assumption that there would be no hours in the Bank at the end of the year, you may roll over the Bank Hours because in some years people will be lucky and not use all of the Banked Hours and in others they will be unlucky and use up more than their Banked Hours. They should oscillate around zero, however they will never have zero.

In this circumstance the Banked Hours should be rolled over.

When a person leaves the company then they should have a deduction in pay if they owe Bank Hours or a payment if they are owed Banked Hours. This is usually based on a pro-rata calculation.

Fairness Criteria

What you want for your members is that any system is fair. To that end you need to ensure that everyone has an equal chance of not using up their Banked Hours and getting the bonus time off.

So, you want an on-call rota. You want the shifts to be numbered so that everyone has an equal chance of being called in. You want to ensure that there can be no favouritism, no nepotism, no bias and that everyone is treated equally.

The only way to ensure this, is if the shift pattern is designed without individuals. Like the shift patterns in this book, people are numbered P1, P2 etc. Then the names are drawn out of a hat and assigned to the rows. Obviously there needs to be some allowances made for skills.

This needs to be done in advance of the shift pattern starting so that everyone can make arrangements for their holidays. Otherwise people will need to do a lot of swapping. We recommend that the shift pattern is issued in October for the following year January to December. If you start the shift pattern at another point, the issue is always the summer holidays. People need to know about summer holidays in the previous autumn if they are to grab the best summer holiday deals.

Call-In Rota

The Call-in Rota has to be specially designed. Firstly, you need to consider how any people should be assigned to each day. This does not mean working out the average number of people who will be absent each day. Absences don't work in that way. We have created a unique book that tells you how many people will be absent each day using a statistical methodology. For example, if you have 10 people on shift for 730 shifts per year (24/7 using 12-hour shifts) and an absence rate of 3%, on average you would have 0.3 of a person missing from each shift or 0.6 of a person missing each day. Under these circumstances you might negotiate for one person to be on-call each day for absences. However, what you would find at the end of the year was that on 538 shifts no one was absent, on 166 shifts one person was absent, on 23 shifts two people were absent and on two shifts three people were absent.

Table 8 shows an estimation of the number of absences per shift over the year for 3% absences and 10 people on shift.

Probability of Absence on Shift   Number of Occasions

No. of Absences	Probability	One Year	Five Years	10 Years
0	0.7374	538	2692	5383
1	0.2281	166	832	1665
2	0.0374	23	116	232
3	0.0026	2	10	19
4	0.0001	0	1	1

Table 8: Statistical Probability of Absence on 730 Shifts

If you look at how many are absent on each day instead. On 198 days no one was absent, on 123 days one person was absent, on 36 days two people were absent, on seven days three people were absent and one day of the year four people were absent.

So, having just one person on call per day is only useful on 123 days. On 44 days or 12% of the time, the operation is running short.

Having four people on call every day for that one day a year is impractical, unless the operation is vital, as in, the company could close for the shift if the person wasn't there or lives were in danger. So, you would probably want either two or three people to be on call each day. You need to weigh up the inconvenience for the people being on-call against the risk of the operation running short.

When it comes to where the cover shifts should be in the rota, you need to think about fatigue and people's holidays. You don't want people to be down to cover for 14-days straight because of the fatigue issues, even if it means that they only have to be on call once a year. Equally you don't want people to be down to be on-call on random days in the middle of their long breaks.

Figures 1,2 and 14,15 & 16 in this book give examples of cover shifts. Here the cover shifts are either single days tagged on to their shifts or they work several cover shifts together.

The on-call rota needs to be as carefully considered as the shift pattern. If you go for the wrong one, it will leave your members exhausted and disillusioned. If you go for a shift pattern that gives them lots of good quality time off and the cover shifts don't interrupt their lives, they will be contented.

In general, people either tend to go with losing two or three long breaks and being on cover instead. This way they get all of their cover over and done within a few weeks. Or they like to work the covers in single days tagged on to the shifts. This means that they don't lose any of their long breaks.

When people are on-call they can still do things. It is not a wasted day. They only need to be available at the start of the shifts. Most of the time they will know well in advance that they are needed.

If they are not needed, they can still do things around the house (laundry, cooking, DIY, gardening etc.) They can still do last minute activities, (gym, day trips, shopping, golf, lunch, cinema etc.). They just can't go away on holiday or make plans they can't cancel.

When you consider that this will only happen on about 15 days per year, it's not too big an imposition is it?

Training

As a union official, you will want the best for your members. Therefore, you want them to have regular training built into the shift pattern. Training means that they stay current with their skills and learn new skills which make them more adaptable and also means that the company is investing in your people.

To that end you need to negotiate that an amount of Banked Hours is set aside for training. Ideally you would want the training shifts to be a full day, limited to 8-hours. No one can learn a new skill for longer than 8-hours. School and university days are limited for this very reason.

The amount of training each person receives should reflect their skill set. Training should also not impinge on the work and make the jobs of the other shift workers harder because they are understaffed. Therefore, it is important that training is covered under the Banked Hours scheme.

Refresher days are important after long breaks when you are dealing with complicated work. Many companies have refresher days when they bring in holidays included shift patterns. On a holidays included pattern it is not uncommon for people to be regularly off work for two or three weeks. Therefore, when they come back to work they not only have to try to remember what they do, after not doing it for an extended period, but they may also have to cope with new procedures and equipment that has been introduced while they were absent. Therefore, the person has a refresher day on the day before their first shift. This may be just 6-hours. So it is not a full shift. Or it may be that they work a 13-hour shift on their first day back and come in an hour earlier to reacquaint themselves with the operation.

Banked Hours are a good way to cover for refresher days, or ad-hoc meetings tagged on to shifts.

Annual Review

When it comes to any form of operation you need to have an annual review. Banked Hours is no different. Every year the company should go through the reasons why they need Banked Hours, make sure that there are enough to cover for all eventualities and that they are still fit for purpose.

Therefore, you should negotiate to have an annual review into Banked Hours to make sure they are still working for everyone.

Shift Swapping

Swapping shifts is an easy way to allow the staff to change their days off, with very little inconvenience to the shift manager. The premise is that if person A is unhappy with the shifts they are scheduled to work e.g. day shift falls on son's birthday so they want to take it as a day off. But if they are on a Holidays Included Shift Pattern so how can they take that day off? Well they swap a shift with one of the other people on the shift pattern who are not working that day shift.

The mechanism for doing this is a shift swapping form. The person who wants a day off asks the other people on the shift pattern if they will be willing to swap that shift. Once they have found someone, they agree between them a like for like swap, which they are both happy with. They then fill in the form and take it to the shift manager to sign. So the staff come to the shift manager with the solution, not the problem. Much better than falling ill on the day and you finding the solution.

On a Holidays Included Shift Pattern, they will all get plenty of time off, and it is very rare that people need particular days off during the year. On a 12-hour shift pattern they will be at work on only $2/5^{ths}$ of the days. So, the occasions when staff will want to swap shifts will be sporadic.

Figure 20 gives an example of a shift swapping form used by many companies. On the left-hand side of the form is the like for like shift swap. This is when two of the shift pattern members agree a like for like swap between them i.e. a Friday Night shift for a Friday Night shift a few weeks later. The right-hand side of the form is for none like for like swaps.

Shift Swapping Request Form

Please complete all sections of the form, sign, and forward to your team manager, no less than 3 days before the start of the shift that is to be swapped. Individual shifts, or stretches of consecutive shifts, can be requested for a swap using this form.

Reference Number:

Y	Y	M	M	D	D	H	H	M	M

Like for Like Shift Swaps *Like for Like Cover Swaps*	*Shift or Cover Swap for a Day Off to Include Changes in Banked Hours*
Requester *(Individual requesting a shift swap)* Name _____	**Requester** *(Individual requesting a shift swap)* Name _____
Original Shift/s or Covers Shift/Cover Date From: _____ To: _____	**Original Shift/s or Covers** Shift Date From: _____ To: _____
New Shift/s or Covers Shift/Cover Date From: _____ To: _____	**Or; New Shift/s or Covers** Date From: _____ To: _____ Hours to the Bank: _____ Or: Hours from the Bank: _____
N.B If individual shifts, please also state whether they are Day or Night	
Requestee *(Individual agreeing to a shift swap)* Name _____	**Requestee** *(Individual agreeing to a shift swap)* Name _____
Original Shift/s or Covers Shift/Cover Date From: _____ To: _____	**Original Shift/s or Covers** Shift Date From: _____ To: _____
New Shift/s or Covers Shift/Cover Date From: _____ To: _____	**Or; New Shift/s or Covers** Shift Date From: _____ To: _____ Hours to the Bank: _____ Or: Hours from the Bank: _____

I agree to the shift change/s stated above, and have made a record of my new shift/s.

Signed *(Requester)* _____

Signed *(Requestee)* _____

Authorised by _____

Figure 20: Example Shift Swap Form

None like for like swaps are where the two people on the shift pattern make a swap but the hours are not the same. An example of this could be on a shift pattern, which uses both 12 and 8-hour shifts. When the swap is not like for like, there will be a discrepancy in the total hours worked for the year. Now these hours have to be accounted for somewhere and one option is the Banked Hours system.

When the swap is not a like for like swap, one person will have to add hours to their bank and the other will remove hours from their hours bank.

Example: Like for Like Shift Swap

	M	T	W	T	F	S	S	M	T	W	T	F	S	S	M	T	W	T	F	S	S	M	T	W	T	F	S	S	M	T	W	T	F	S	S
Alan T	D	D	N	N					D	D	N	N	N									D	D	D	N	N									
Faith S			D	D	N	N	N				D	D	D	N	N															D	D	N	N		
Hailey A								D	D	D	N	N										D	D	N	N								D	D	N	N
Carlton F	N	N										D	D	N	N						D	D	N	N	N									D	D	D
Barry L								D	D	N	N							D	D	N	N	N								D	D	D	N	N	
Days	1	1	1	1	1	1	1	1	1	1	1	1	1	1	1	1	1	1	1	1	1	1	1	1	1	1	1	1	1	1	1	1	1	1	1
Nights	1	1	1	1	1	1	1	1	1	1	1	1	1	1	1	1	1	1	1	1	1	1	1	1	1	1	1	1	1	1	1	1	1	1	1

Figure 21: Five week shift pattern 554 holidays included

In this example there are five people working a holidays included 554 pattern. They receive their shift pattern for the year and everything is going ok then a few months in Hailey finds out that she needs to have those highlighted 3 day shifts off. So how can she take those three day shifts off? Well she just has to do a swap with one of the other people not working on those days.

She can't swap with Alan because he is working a Night shift before those day shifts. She can't swap with Faith because she is working the night shift on those days. But she can swap with Carlton or Barry. So Hailey phones up Barry, but he can't work those shifts because he has plans, so then she calls Carlton and he says yes, he can work those shifts. Now they need a like for like swap, and Carlton is not particularly pleased to be working the three night shifts a couple of weeks later, so he proposes that they swap those shifts and Hailey agrees.

They then fill in the form and take it to the shift manager for authorisation. The filled in form is shown in figure 20. Figure 22 shows the new shift pattern worked by the staff.

	M	T	W	T	F	S	S	M	T	W	T	F	S	S	M	T	W	T	F	S	S	M	T	W	T	F	S	S	M	T	W	T	F	S	S
Alan T	D	D	N	N					D	D	N	N	N									D	D	D	N	N									
Faith S			D	D	N	N	N				D	D	D	N	N															D	D	N	N		
Hailey A									N	N												D	D	N	N	N	N	N					D	D	N	N
Carlton F	N	N			D	D	D					D	D	N	N						D	D												D	D	D
Barry L								D	D	N	N							D	D	N	N	N								D	D	D	N	N	
Days	1	1	1	1	1	1	1	1	1	1	1	1	1	1	1	1	1	1	1	1	1	1	1	1	1	1	1	1	1	1	1	1	1	1	1
Nights	1	1	1	1	1	1	1	1	1	1	1	1	1	1	1	1	1	1	1	1	1	1	1	1	1	1	1	1	1	1	1	1	1	1	1

Figure 22: The 554 pattern after the shift swap

In figure 22 you will note that Hailey is now no longer working the three day shifts in week 1. Carlton is now working those day shifts and Carlton is no longer working the night shifts in week 4; they have been moved to Hailey.

Shift Swapping Request Form

Please complete all sections of the form, sign, and forward to your team manager, no less than 3 days before the start of the shift that is to be swapped. Individual shifts, or stretches of consecutive shifts, can be requested for a swap using this form.

Reference Number:

Y	Y	M	M	D	D	H	H	M	M
0	8	0	2	0	1	1	4	2	5

Like for Like Shift Swaps *Like for Like Cover Swaps*	*Shift or Cover Swap for a Day Off to Include Changes in Banked Hours*
Requester *(Individual requesting a shift swap)* Name Hailey A	**Requester** *(Individual requesting a shift swap)* Name _____
Original Shift/s or Covers Shift/Cover Date From: ___07/03___ To: ___09/03___	**Original Shift/s or Covers** Shift Date From: _____ To: _____
New Shift/s or Covers Shift/Cover Date From: ___28/03___ To: ___30/03___	**Or; New Shift/s or Covers** Date From: _____ To: _____ Hours to the Bank: _____ Or: Hours from the Bank: _____

N.B If individual shifts, please also state whether they are Day or Night

Requestee *(Individual agreeing to a shift swap)* Name Carlton F	**Requestee** *(Individual agreeing to a shift swap)* Name _____
Original Shift/s or Covers Shift/Cover Date From: ___28/03___ To: ___30/03___	**Original Shift/s or Covers** Shift Date From: _____ To: _____
New Shift/s or Covers Shift/Cover Date From: ___07/03___ To: ___09/03___	**Or; New Shift/s or Covers** Shift Date From: _____ To: _____ Hours to the Bank: _____ Or: Hours from the Bank: _____

I agree to the shift change/s stated above, and have made a record of my new shift/s.

Signed *(Requester)* _____

Signed *(Requestee)* _____

Authorised by _____

© C-Desk Technology 01636 816466 The Old Vicarage, Rolleston, Newark, Notts, UK NG23 5SE email: alec@visualrota.co.uk www.visualrota.co.uk

Figure 23: Shift Swapping form filled out by Hailey and Carlton

Example: Shift Swapping which includes Changes to Banked Hours

	M	T	W	T	F	S	S	M	T	W	T	F	S	S	M	T	W	T	F	S	S	M	T	W	T	F	S	S	M	T	W	T	F	S	S
Mary A	D	D			N	N	N		D	D					N	N		D	D	D			N	N											
Pete V			D	D				N	N			D	D	D		N	N												D	D				N	N
Simon T	N	N			D	D	D			N	N							D	D		N	N	N			D	D								
Charlotte E		N	N										D	D		N	N	N		D	D			N	N					D	D	D			
Michel B						D	D				N	N	N		D	D			N	N			D	D	D			N	N						
Days	1	1	1	1	1	1	1	1	1	1	1	1	1	1	1	1	1	1	1	1	1	1	1	1	1	1	1	1	1	1	1	1	1	1	1
Nights	1	1	1	1	1	1	1	1	1	1	1	1	1	1	1	1	1	1	1	1	1	1	1	1	1	1	1	1	1	1	1	1	1	1	1

Figure 24: Five week shift pattern 232 holidays included

In this example there are five people working a 232 pattern holidays included. Pete wants to take the three day shifts scheduled in week 2 off. To get those three days off he has to swap with either Mary or Charlotte. Mary is willing to swap those three day shifts for the two night shifts the following week. Pete agrees and they fill out the form and take it to the shift manager for authorisation. The filled in form is shown in figure 26. Because the three day shifts are not the same number of hours as the two night shifts, they have to fill out the right-hand side of the form and there is a change in their Banked Hours. Since the shifts are 12-hours long Mary's Banked Hours are reduced by 12-hours, and Pete's Banked Hours are increased by 12-hours.

Figure 25 shows the new shift pattern worked by the staff.

	M	T	W	T	F	S	S	M	T	W	T	F	S	S	M	T	W	T	F	S	S	M	T	W	T	F	S	S	M	T	W	T	F	S	S
Mary A	D	D			N	N	N		D	D	D	D				D	D	D					N	N											
Pete V			D	D				N	N						N	N	N	N											D	D				N	N
Simon T	N	N			D	D	D			N	N							D	D		N	N	N			D	D								
Charlotte E		N	N										D	D		N	N	N		D	D			N	N					D	D	D			
Michel B						D	D				N	N	N		D	D			N	N			D	D	D			N	N						
Days	1	1	1	1	1	1	1	1	1	1	1	1	1	1	1	1	1	1	1	1	1	1	1	1	1	1	1	1	1	1	1	1	1	1	1
Nights	1	1	1	1	1	1	1	1	1	1	1	1	1	1	1	1	1	1	1	1	1	1	1	1	1	1	1	1	1	1	1	1	1	1	1

Figure 25: The 232 pattern after the shift swap

In figure 25 you will note that Pete is now no longer working the three day shifts in week 2. Mary is now working those day shifts. And Mary is no longer working the night shifts in week 3; they have been moved to Pete.

Shift Swapping Request Form

Please complete all sections of the form, sign, and forward to your team manager, no less than 3 days before the start of the shift that is to be swapped. Individual shifts, or stretches of consecutive shifts, can be requested for a swap using this form.

Reference Number:

Y	Y	M	M	D	D	H	H	M	M
0	6	0	7	0	3	0	9	4	5

Like for Like Shift Swaps **Like for Like Cover Swaps**	**Shift or Cover Swap for a Day Off to Include Changes in Banked Hours**
Requester (Individual requesting a shift swap) Name _____	*Requester* (Individual requesting a shift swap) Name Pete V
Original Shift/s or Covers Shift/Cover Date From: _____ To: _____	**Original Shift/s or Covers** Shift Date From: ___08/09___ To: ___10/09___
New Shift/s or Covers Shift/Cover Date From: _____ To: _____	**Or; New Shift/s or Covers** Date From: ___11/09___ To: ___12/09___ Hours to the Bank: __12__ Or: Hours from the Bank: _____
N.B If individual shifts, please also state whether they are Day or Night	
Requestee (Individual agreeing to a shift swap) Name _____	*Requestee* (Individual agreeing to a shift swap) Name Mary A
Original Shift/s or Covers Shift/Cover Date From: _____ To: _____	**Original Shift/s or Covers** Shift Date From: ___11/09___ To: ___12/09___
New Shift/s or Covers Shift/Cover Date From: _____ To: _____	**Or; New Shift/s or Covers** Shift Date From: ___08/09___ To: ___10/09___ Hours to the Bank: _____ Or: Hours from the Bank: __12__

I agree to the shift change/s stated above, and have made a record of my new shift/s.

Signed *(Requester)* _____

Signed *(Requestee)* _____

Authorised by _____

© C-Desk Technology 01636 816466 The Old Vicarage, Rolleston, Newark, Notts, UK NG23 5SE email: alec@visualrota.co.uk www.visualrota.co.uk

Figure 26: Shift Swapping form filled out by Pete and Mary

Countries Setting Maximum Weekly Hours

Some countries set the maximum contracted weekly hours. This is often set at 40 hours per week and any additional hours worked in that week have to be additional hours and paid at overtime rates.

At first glance, this would seem to be at odds with having flexible hours since working fewer hours in one week will cause them to work more hours in another week.

There would appear to be only a few shifts and a few shift patterns that can provide a stable flat operation. 40 hours in a week would appear to mean that you could only use 8-hour shifts. We have created shift patterns using 10-hour shifts, but there are problems creating teams when the workload is flat. 10-hour shifts work well when the workload is variable over the day.

However, the main point at issue is that a legal framework limiting the week to 40-hours means that Banked Hours would be paid as overtime, and then all the usual rules can apply. It is cheaper to pay overtime and be able to bring in the required resources than to run short or to over-staff on every shift. So they are effectively contracted for 40+ hours

Office Workers

We have set up operations for lots of different offices. We tend to find that many offices have a variable workload over the day. Most no longer work the typically 9-5 operation. Many like to have an 7-7 operational period. This means that people who come in early can ensure that everything is ready for when their main workload starts at 9am. Then people are there later to ensure that client problems are dealt with the same day even if the work comes in at 4 or 5 pm.

Having a 12-hour window for the working day means that employees can vary their hours according to their personal circumstances. So if they have an appointment, then they can leave work early or arrive at work late and still complete their normal hours.

Shifts for the Office

For most people they don't have a choice as to when or how often they come into work. They work 9-5 every Monday to Friday, because that is the accepted arrangement. However, it doesn't have to be this way. When companies start thinking outside of the traditional office "box" they find that there is a host of options they never considered.

Not all of our clients are big factories, hospitals, large utilities all operating 24/7. Very often our clients are offices trying to maximise efficiency and create a better work/life balance. We have set up lots of call centres that operate Monday-Friday or Monday to Saturday. Engineers, IT, NOC, SOC, Technician, Administration, gyms, community care workers etc. There are lots of jobs that still revolve around Monday-Friday with extended working hours. Some even have an on-call service over night in case of an emergency, yet their core business is still very office hours based.

In the UK the average commute is 29 minutes. Which means that if you work for five days per week, then you are stuck commuting for an average 4 hours and 50 minutes per week. If you take into account holidays (5.6 weeks per year) and a week of sickness per year, then you are looking at spending about 220 hours per year commuting to and from work. On a 37.5-hour contract that's over 11% of your contracted hours per year.

So if you work just 9-hour (8.5h paid) shifts instead of 8-hour (7.5h paid) shifts on 37.5 hours per week, you would save about 25 hours of commutes per year. Then there is the petrol or train fares to consider. So working longer days means big savings.

Once you start down the longer shifts route, you can get better operations. You can match the shifts to the workload. So if there is a peak in the middle of the day, you can overlap the early and late shifts to meet it.

An important part of extending working hours is ensuring fairness with late working, weekend cover or on-calls. Setting up a shift pattern is not just about making sure that the workload is covered. It's about ensuring that everyone is fairly treated, that you won't be asked to be on-call every Christmas. That you get the same number of weekends off as everyone else.

If shifts are longer than 8-hours it's also about ensuring that everyone has the same number of days off. Working shifts in an office environment makes a lot of sense. You maintain complete control over the operation, you can have less space in the office, be available to clients outside of 9-5 and because people have days off, they can come in and cover for absences.

Extending office hours has many benefits to the company and their employees. From the company perspective, they can guarantee that people will be in the office over a greater period of time, guaranteeing services outside of traditional hours. This may be sold to prestigious clients only. Their employees can also do work outside of traditional office hours. So if a job comes in at 5pm and it takes four hours to complete, it can be ready for 9am the following working day, thus exceeding your service level expectations. The company can also match the staffing levels to the workload. Thus, reducing wastage and increasing profits. The commuting time of the employees is also reduced; thus, they are less fatigued and make fewer mistakes. They may also be healthier and happier as a result of the reduced stress and commuting time. The company is also greener as a result.

Extending office hours gives the employees more time at home, less time stuck in traffic and more quality time off. Their holidays are nearly doubled by just working an hour extra each day. They can also spend time doing work when they are not interacting with the public. Thus, reducing their stress and they get to commute outside of the rush hour.

How Flexi Time Works

Flexi time allows the employee to work at a time of their choosing within the company's rules. This means that by working more hours together, they can have more time off together. They are perfectly entitled to extra days off. This is because they do work their contracted hours, hence they are fulfilling their contract and doing the work they are being paid for.

What is important when introducing Flexi Time is that the work is not time critical. By that I do not mean that they don't have to meet deadlines. Rather, that their work is just as effective if they did it on Tuesday rather than Monday or if they did the work at 7am rather than 10am. So it would be inappropriate for call centres or production where other people are relying on a continuous flow.

To introduce Flexi Time you need core hours, these are hours when the people can work effectively. So you might go for a 12-hour window for example 7am-7pm Monday to Friday. So people can start and finish anytime during that period. You may also want to have a compulsory period when people are most effective for instance 10am-2pm. This means that the person has to start work between 7am and 10am. They can also finish work between 2pm and 7pm. This way you would schedule meetings within the 10am-2pm window.

If a person works 7am-7pm then they would effectively be working for 12-hours. If they were on 37-hours per week, then they would only have to work 25 hours over the rest of the week. If they did one 9-hour day and two 8-hour days, they could have a day off. Normally managers would have to sign off on a whole day off and people might be restricted to so many days off per year.

The advantages to the individual for having Flexi time are immense:

- There is the better work/life balance, they can tailor their working time to match in with their lifestyle.
- They can have days off and therefore less commutes. The average commute within the UK is 29 minutes, so if they had 10 extra days off each year they would save nearly 10 hours a year in commutes.
- The operation is less fatiguing for people, if you have to commute in rush hour, then you are likely stressed and

exhausted when you arrive. The same for your journey home. However by commuting outside of rush hour you can reduce your fatigue. You can also reduce your stress because if you have to leave work for an appointment or to pick up your children, you can without taking a day off work.

- More days off mean more time with family and friends. Even if they are working during the week you can still do all of those household jobs during the week when shops are less busy and then enjoy your weekends.
- If you are not feeling well at work, or just a bit under the weather, with Flexi time you could go in later or go home early, or just request the day off. This means that you are generally healthier, because you can respond quicker to illness.

The advantages to the company for having Flexi time are just as good:

- Better motivated workers, because they are happier they tend to be more motivated to get the job done well
- Your operation is more effective and efficient. Imagine you have an important deadline looming, instead of asking people to work overtime, they can just have TOIL (Time Off In Lieu) instead at a time of their choosing
- If people are suffering fatigue because of their home lives (maybe their child is sick or they have to take care of a relative) then they could work shorter days or even a day off without wasting holidays. Then work longer days when they can to make up their hours. This means that overall people are less fatigued at work. Therefore they are less prone to making errors.
- If not everyone is coming in everyday then you need less facilities. If everyone was on flexi time, time you might only have 80% in each day. This means they you could have 20% less office space, 20% less car parking spaces, 20% less computers etc. This results in huge savings as the hot desking and working from home initiatives show. Yet with Flexi Time you have all the advantages of home working and all of the advantages of office working because people are still coming into the office. So they still mix with each other, they still attend meetings in person, and they can still be home for the plumber.

- Flexi Time often results in lower sickness rates. This is especially true if there is an attendance bonus. If people can get to the doctors quicker because they can just leave work early to get to an appointment, then they tend to be healthier. Catching an illness quicker frequently means less recovery time. The vast majority of sickness is caused by skeletal problems, cold/flu or mental health. With cold and flu the ability to take days off means that the rest of the office don't catch it thus reducing overall sickness. With skeletal problems the faster they are dealt with the better and reducing stress along with a better worklife balance will help their mental health.

Put that way, the question is why isn't everyone doing it?

When appropriate we promote Flexi Time to our clients because of the benefits to both parties. The disadvantages are limited to a reduction in overtime to the employee and the company needs to ensure that the system is not abused. That is why it's important that all days off are signed off by the managers.

Unlimited Holidays

Some organisations have introduced unlimited holidays. On the face of it when you first hear it this sounds great. However this does tend to throw up a few issues.

One company had people scheduled to work every day of the year. Then if you didn't want to come in, you didn't have to, you just weren't paid for that day. It's like an extreme contractor. Work as many days as you like.

The problem comes with if they are working 24/7 how do they go from nights to days? You end up needing quick turn arounds which are not great for rest so they need to do it infrequently.

A combination of Flexi Time and Job and Knock would work for office workers if the work wasn't time critical. Then they could have as much time off as they wanted provided they got their work completed on time.

However if you allow people to have as much time off as they want or as much time off as their work allows, how much holiday have they taken?

What happens if someone can't take any holiday because their workload doesn't allow it? What happens if they are on Banked

Hours and have lots of time off anyway so that they don't need their holidays?

If you allow people to take holidays only if they want to or if the work allows, then some people might not take any holiday. It is the responsibility of the company in the UK and Europe to ensure that all of its employees have the opportunity to take holidays. This responsibility cannot be delegated to the individual. This often results in people being forced off on holiday.

Therefore before you decide that unlimited holidays could work for you. You need a way of recording the holidays and ensuring that if you are in the UK then everyone takes the minimum 5.6 weeks.

It is also worth ensuring that people take a mandatory two week break each year. This is a good way to ensure that they are doing their job. Traditionally, Banks always ensured that everyone had a two-week break so that they could not defraud the Bank. If you scheduled these in and people took a two week break in turn you can ensure fair dealing across all operations.

Summary

In operations that require assured continuity of staffing and where overtime is an inappropriate means of delivering the assurance, the system of Banked Hours has evolved to provide it. It has to be flexible in operation and fair to the staff in operation by minimising any disruptions to the staff. Banked Hours is not a system specifically designed to reduce the hours worked by the staff, even though that is usually the case, and this also incentivises employees into approving the Banked Hours system.

Reasons for using Banked Hours;

- Absence Cover
- Training
- Legal Leave
- Leavers
- Ad-hoc Work

The reward structure;

- Payment in Advance
- Overtime Rates
- Time Off In Lieu (TOIL)
- Basic Rates + Shift Allowance
- Extra Time off if hours are unutilised
- Early Retirement

Banked Hours can be used on 8 and 12-hour shifts. You need to have a different approach to using Banked Hours when you are on 8-hour shifts to when you are on 12-hour shifts. When on 8-hour shifts, the usual method is to use Banked Hours to extend the shift to 12-hours and cover for absences that way. On 12-hour shifts the usual method is to have cover shifts on their days off and then use the Banked hours to pay for them when needed.

The uses an organisation wants to put the Bank Hours to, determine the number of Banked Hours. Each of these is calculated separately.

Banked hours work well for the company and the shift workers provided it is not abused. Banked Hours should be seen as a privilege.

Calculation Example

Shift Pattern requires:	1800 hours/year/employee
3% absence rate	54 hours of absence each on average
Authorised leave	10 hours/year/person
Training	40 hours/year/person
Ad-hoc work	24 hours/year/person
25-33% on absences	18 hours/year/person
Total required	146 hours/year/person

Recruitment

It's a small world these days, and it's as well to remember that.

There will come a time when you have to recruit a new person onto the rota, and you have to sell 'Banked Hours'. How will you describe the benefits? How will you describe the 'fair and equitable' cover rota, the means of calling people in and their reward?

It's easy to sell to a new manager: Well we have a fully staffed operation. You never have to worry about absence problems, so you are free to concentrate on the business side. This operation is a tried and tested system, the staff love it, so just keep everything going.

Now think about selling it to a new machine operator, or call centre operator, a line worker or warehouse operative:

"Our policy is to ensure that everyone achieves a good work/life balance. To this end we use a flexible approach to staffing. We ensure that all of our shifts are fully staffed. Our shift pattern is based around creating a stable environment for our shift workers. Our policies prevent nepotism, favoritism, harassment or bullying. We like to think of our team as a family. We actively encourage cross team integration through our cover shift program."

When it comes to flexible shift work it is not enough to just have one tool at your disposal. A good manager needs lots of tools available for all eventualities. A good manager will have backup plans for alternative scenarios thus they will never have to firefight.

Banked Hours is great to managing flexibility and improving shift worker's work/life balance. However, you should run a Banked Hours system with at least a few other flexible tools.

Variable Shift Lengths increase flexibility and can be used with "Job and Knock", time off in lieu and U-shifts. This means that you can offer stability and flexibility to your shift workers and improve their work/life balance.

Shift Swapping is key for any flexible arrangement. It cost little or nothing to implement. However, the rewards are huge when it comes to employees' moral and their work/life balance. All you need is a shift swapping form.

If you want to run a flexible operation, then you need to think about multi skilling. The more people you have with the same skills, the more flexible your operation becomes. If everyone can cover for everyone else, then they have more people to swap with, you have more resources available and you end up with a more efficient and stable operation.

The traditional approach to flexible shift working, is when you run short and use overtime. If you can use these tools strategically, you will have an efficient and flexible operation. However, most of the time it is miss used and results in high costs, little flexibility and a poor work/life balance. This is often due to not understanding the fundamental principles involved in successful Banked Hour operations.

Work/life Balance

"What is a good work/life balance?"

Defining a work/life balance is easy, however what is a good one is subjective. Everyone talks about achieving a good work/life balance. So here is what I think of as a good work/life balance:

When at work: you want to know when you will be needed to work with sufficient notice and the work to be unfatiguing i.e. not stressful, varied, interesting, not overworked or underworked

When at home: you want to have good quality time away from work, between sets of consecutive shifts a few days is required to fully recover. Between shifts you need a minimum of 11 hours so that you can have a good quality rest. When on holiday you need regular time off for a minimum of five days.

When on-call: You don't want to have work being able to contact you every moment you are not at work, in case there is an emergency and you are needed. So, create contingency plans into the shift schedule right up front. This means that everyone knows when they could be contacted, the probability of being contacted at any time and how to ensure they are not contacted when they don't want to be.

This is what I mean by a shift schedule that gives you a good work/life balance. So, when you are creating your shift pattern, keep these ideals in mind and ask yourself is this creating a good work/life balance for my employees?

Create shift schedules for a year in advance, so your shift workers always know when you expect them to be at work. The shift schedule should minimise fatigue, allow them to live their life while away from work without any work worries and maintain the operation so that the company can maximise profits, so their job is never in danger.

Glossary

2-shift System – A shift system consisting of early and late shifts (Monday – Friday)

3-shift System – A shift system consisting of early, late and night shifts (Monday – Friday)

4-shift System - A shift system consisting of early, late and night shifts seven days a week

10-hour Shift - A nominal elapsed period of time of 10 hours during which staff have to attend work

Absence - The state of being away or not present

Afternoon Shift - A shift that has a substantial period of time after noon

Annual Shutdowns – A period when the plant is closed and staff are expected to use some of their holidays

Annualised Hours – Everything is calculated on a yearly basis

Bank Holidays - Holidays that are annually set by the Government but have no legal status

Banked Hours – A system of pre-paid hours, usually contractual

Breaks - A period of rest time between periods of work time

C – A rostered Cover period in a shift pattern, may be for: 8 hours, 12 hours, 24 hours, or multiples of these

Calendar Year - A period of time set by the company containing 12 calendar months

Call In – Same as Call Out

Call Out– A system that has a person who is not scheduled to work, come to work

Company Year - A period of time set by the company containing 12 calendar months

Cover – Where a person is resting at home but scheduled to work if an absence occurs

Cover Period – The continuous period of time that one person is on Cover, or a group of staff are on Cover

Day - A 24 hour period or one fifth of a working week, or a period of time when the sun is above the horizon

Day Shift – A shift, which has approximately equal periods of time before and after noon or a nominal name given to shifts that occupy notional office hours

Early Shift – A shift that has a substantial period of time before noon

Employee - One who works, someone to whom an employer has a duty to provide work

Employer - A person who employs

End of Year - After the year has finished

Evening Shift - A nominal name given to shifts that finish in the Evening

Fatigue – A mental condition, which reduces the effectiveness of the person

Flat Staffing Levels – Where the same number of people are required to work at all times

Flexed Shifts – A means of standing people down during quiet periods and bringing them in during busy periods

Floating Days – A system on a HISP where people can pick additional days of holiday

Frequency of Cover – The number of times in a year that a person is on Cover, sometimes in absolute units, sometimes in combinations of units of Cover. For instance a person can be on Cover for 48-hour periods 6 times a year, or 24-hour periods 12 times a year

Golden Days – A system on a HISP where people can pick additional days of holiday

HESP – Holiday Excluded Shift Pattern – where staff request holidays

HISP – Holiday Included Shift Pattern – where holidays are an integral part of the shift pattern

HISP232 – Shift pattern based on shifts worked in 2's & 3's with special regard for working weekends. May be 8-hour or 12-hour shifts

HISP DDNN – 12-hour Shift pattern based on working 4 shifts as 2 Days + 2 Nights

Holiday - Time that is paid by an employer but is not worked by the employee

Holiday Carry Over - If staff do not take all of their annual holiday entitlement in one year, some companies allow their entitlement to be carried over to the next year

Holiday Management Plan – A system to manage the holidays in accordance with the holiday resources

Holiday Quotas – A holiday management plan to spread holidays evenly throughout the year

Holiday Resource – The number of over staffed shifts available for holiday cover in a year

Holiday Year - A period of time set by the company containing 12 calendar months during which the company must make provision for all staff to take their holiday entitlement

Internal Body Clock – An internal mechanism by which the body functions are regulated

Late Shift– See afternoon shift

Leap Year - A year containing 366 days

Leaver - A person who leaves part way through a year

Long Term Absence Notification – Absences notified with greater than 24-hours' notice, typically the second and subsequent day of absence

Migration Plan – A system to move people from one shift pattern to a new shift pattern

Morning Shift – See early shift

Normal Hours - Hours normally worked by an employee in the course of performing their duties

Night Shift – A shift, which has a substantial period of time between 1 a.m. and 5 a.m.

Night Time - A period of at least seven hours which includes the period from midnight to 5 a.m. that can be determined by a relevant agreement. In the absence of such an agreement it will be 11 p.m. to 6 a.m.

Night Workers - A night worker is any worker whose daily working time includes at least 3 hours of night time

Office Hours – Monday to Friday 9 a.m. till 5 p.m.

On-call– A system where a person is available to work if necessary

Overtime – Payment for hour worked in excess of a persons contracted hours

Pareto Principle – 80/20 rule, the law of vital few and the principle of factor scarcity states that for many events, 80% of the effects come from 20% of the causes

Pro rata - In proportion

Public Holiday – Statuary Holidays, or State Holidays

Rest Time – A period of not working between shifts

Reward Structure – The reason why people come to work

Roll Over - Is the action of a shift pattern, which ignores the end of year, and continue from one year to the next

Round Robin – Calling up everyone on a list

Service Level Agreements – The quality of a service the organisation guarantees

Shift – A period of time during which a shift worker is at the disposal of the organisation, it is never a body of men in this book

Shift Allowance - A premium, which companies pay to employees as compensation for working unsocial hours

Shift Pattern - A regular pattern of shifts that all staff on the shift pattern will work in turn

Shift Roster - A set of shifts that an employee will work

Shift Rota - A set of shifts that an employee will work

Shift System - A shift pattern that uses one group of staff to work shifts, typically, an Early, Late and Night shift, to a rotation

Shift Table – A table detailing the start and finish times of all shifts in a week

Short Term Absence Notification – Absences notified with less than 24 hours notice

Sickness Leave - Absence from work by an employee claiming they are unfit to work

Skill – Refers to a level of expertise, responsibility, which requires training time

Stand-by – A system, which allows managers to call in a worker from home to cover for absence

Starters - A person who starts part way through a year

Statuary Holidays - Annual leave specified by law

Terms of Employment – A contract between the employer and the employee detailing what is expected for all parties

Time off – Time when employees are not at the disposal of the organisation

TOIL – Time Off In Lieu, a system of allowing the same, or greater, amount of time off at another time

TOUP – Train Once Use Plenty

Types of Leave - Absence from work by an employee for reasons other than sickness or holiday, e.g., Maternity, Paternity, Bereavement, and Sabbaticals

U Shift - Unallocated shift requiring staff to attend for work at specified times for unspecified duties, often used to cover for absences

Variable Staffing Levels – The variation in the number of staff required to be at work at anytime

Week – A period of 168 hours such as Monday 7 a.m. till Monday 7 a.m. or a period seven consecutive days, or the five days Monday to Friday, or a contracted number of hours a person is required to work

Weekend - A period of time from a Friday or Saturday to a Monday morning

Worker - One who works, someone to whom an employer has a duty to provide work

Working Time - When a worker is working, at his employer's disposal and carrying out his activity or duties

Workload – The number of hours x the number of people required to do the work

Year - A period of time determined by the period of rotation of the Earth around the Sun. A year is 52 weeks, or 52 weeks and 1/7 of a week (52 $2/7$ weeks every leap year) or 52 weeks if 31st December falls on a Saturday or Sunday or 52 $1/5$ weeks if 31st December falls Monday to Friday. (if a leap year then a year is 52 $2/5$ weeks if 30th December falls on Monday to Friday)

Authors

Alec Jezewski

Alec Jezewski graduated from UMIST with a degree in Mechanical Engineering. He then went on to do post graduate research at Nottingham Trent University setting up computer models for high-pressure gas cylinders. Afterwards Alec joined Rolls Royce in the Stress Office for several years. His speciality was creating computer models to compare theoretical design with real structures. He left in 1985 to start his own 24/365 business.

In 1994 Alec Jezewski founded CDT to help organisations write their shift patterns. The idea was born in his mind after watching his wife struggle to write shift patterns for their 24 hour 365 days per year business. Being an engineer he decided that there had to be a logical approach to shift pattern design and a way to run the shift pattern effectively. What he found was that there was very little literature on the subject and most of this was contradicting and non-practical.

Now after more than 25 years in the field he not only helps create shift patterns for companies but he also advises clients on how to define workload, select a shift pattern, organise cover arrangement, shift allowances, advise staff on fatigue, writes employment rules and negotiates with unions.

He has worked with companies all around the world including Australia, USA, Canada, and Europe. Many of his clients are companies from abroad who have UK based operations. Companies he works for range from the very largest to small offices.

Dr Angela Moore

In 2001 Angela Moore joined CDT. Angela has a Doctorate from Southampton University in Management creating statistical models. An MSc in Operations Management from Manchester Business School where her dissertation was on comparing shift patterns used in the public and private sectors. A BSc from UMIST in Mathematics, Statistics and Operational Research where her final year thesis was modelling call centre workloads.

Being a mathematician and statistician Angela has assisted companies improving their overall shift pattern designs, define their workload and run operations more effectively. She has designed several software packages to help create and manage shift patterns including VisualrotaX.

Angela's statistical analysis techniques have enabled organisations to put in very cost effective and efficient absence and holiday cover arrangements. By assessing absence statistics, she has enabled companies to analyse their absences to predict when staff will be absence and provide cover accordingly.

Angela has advanced the rather crude Erlang's equations for call centres, the most frequently used method of analysis in predicting staffing requirements, to include new equations that cover real events (meal and rest breaks, queues, dropped calls, redials, etc.). Location analysis is a new field, whereby the location of goods within a warehouse or jobs around the country can contribute significantly to the efficiency of an operation. Angela's analysis gives great insight into the way that organisations can organise maintenance work, repair work, emergency services and the location of new facilities.

Clients

We work for organisations around the world and in every industry. Today, everyone expects businesses to operate 24/7. They want to be served to their agenda, hence there is increasing pressure to be open longer. We help our clients meet expectations. Our shift patterns allow them to make more, serve more and do more with optimum efficiency.

Public Sector

10 Downing St., Aber University, Anglian Water, BBC, Bedford NHS Trust, Bedfordshire Police, Bradford City Council, Bradford University, Britannia Building Society, Durham Aycliffe, Essex Police, Glasgow City, Glasgow Diocese, Glasgow Museums, University of Hertfordshire, Homefirst, Hounslow, University of Kent, Hillcroft College, Hounslow, Jersey, Kensington & Chelsea, Kings College, Kingston, Land Registry, Leeds Met Uni, London Transport Museum, Mansfield, Merton, Metropolitan Police,Millennium Dome, Nottingham City Hospital, Nottinghamshire CC, Plymouth Uni, Royal Cornwall Hospitals,

Royal Hospital Chelsea, Sedgefield, Sheffield Uni, SOCA, Staffordshire Police, Sutton, Warwickshire Police, Yell,

Private Sector

ACR, Acora, ADM Milling, Amscott, APX, Arriva, Ashfield Homes, At the Races, Bakkavor, Barclays Bank, Barr, Biffa, Birds, BP, British American Tobacco, Coors, CSM, Daily Mirror, Dairy Crest, DFDS, Diageo, Discovery TV, Dulux, Dunlop, Financial Times, George King, Graham & Brown, H3G, Holmesterne, Howdens, HSBC, Huntsman, ICI, Ideal World, Immingham Port, Independent Newspapers, IPN, ITC, Johnson Matthey, Kingspan, Lebara, LNWR, London Imaging, Marlow Foods, Martin Baker, Mitie, National Grid, New Wave, NIE, NWG, Nymas, Pearson, Peel Ports, PPG, Premier Foods, Protherics, PW Defence, Rascal, RBS Bank, Runtech, Sca Nutech, Scottish Power, Smith Nephew, SSE, Style Group, Suttons, TrekAmerica, Turbine Services, Twinnings, United Biscuits, Wagg Foods, Warburtons, Worldwide Fruit., Yell, Yorkshire Water

International

6 Continents Hotels, AAK, ABB, Alstom, Bermuda Police, Bord Gais, Cabot, Coca-Cola, Coors, Croda, CSM, Digital Shadows, Dupont, Engie, ESB, Eutelsat, ExxonMobile, Firmenich, Fuji Film, Gilead, Greif, Guenther, Heidelberg, Hutchinson, ICE, Inco, Intergen, Johns Manville, Kalmar, KWE, Lonza, McCain, McCormick, Mondi, NCR, Nestle, Nicepak, Nisshinbo Group, Novartis, NPower, Nymas, Oman Cables, Onyx, RaboBank, Raytheon, Reed Hycalog, Research in Motion, Schlumberger, Schrader, Schutz, St Gobain, Stanley,TAG, Ticona, Tradebe, Zund

Further Reading

AJ Operations Consulting, 2001, Shift Pattern Parameters.

Jezewska Angela, 2001, Stochastic Models for Simulation of Call Centres.

Jezewska Angela, 2002, Compare and Contrast Public and Private Sector Staffing Forecasts

Jezewski Alec, Moore Angela, 2008, How to Manage your Shift Pattern

Other books in the Shift Pattern Tools & Techniques series:

- Holidays Excluded Shift Pattern
- Holidays Included Shift Pattern
- Holiday Management Plan
- Calculating How Many Staff You Need
- Shift Cover Arrangements
- Fatigue & Shift Work
- Incorporating Training
- Terms & Conditions of Employment
- Staff Questions
- Workload Analysis
- Calculating Shift Allowances
- Check List
- Creating a Shift Pattern

www.ingramcontent.com/pod-product-compliance
Lightning Source LLC
Chambersburg PA
CBHW072207290526
45794CB00004B/1683